THE ROAD TO REDEMPTION

Other Books by Burton L. Visotzky
The Genesis of Ethics
Reading the Book

THE ROAD TO REDEMPTION

*Lessons from Exodus
on Leadership and Community*

BURTON L. VISOTZKY

Crown Publishers, Inc. • *New York*

Published by Crown Publishers, Inc., 201 East 50th Street, New York,
New York 10022. Member of the Crown Publishing Group.

Random House, Inc. New York, Toronto, London, Sydney, Auckland
www.randomhouse.com

CROWN and colophon are trademarks of Crown Publishers, Inc.

Printed in the United States of America

Design by Cynthia Dunne

LIBRARY OF CONGRESS CATALOGING-IN-PUBLICATION DATA
Visotzky, Burton L.
    The road to redemption : lessons from Exodus on leadership and
community / Burton L. Visotzky. — 1st ed.
    1. Bible. O.T. Exodus — Criticism, interpretation, etc.
    2. Leadership in the Bible.   3. Community — Biblical teaching.
    4. Visotzky, Burton L.   I. Title.
    BS1245.6.L42V57   1998
    222'.1206—dc21   98–6252
                                                                   CIP

ISBN 0–609–60145–8

10 9 8 7 6 5 4 3 2 1

First Edition

*For the Visotzky, Berk,
and now Edelman clans
—my family—
with love.*

CONTENTS

The Great Stories are the ones you have heard and want to hear again. The ones you can enter anywhere and inhabit comfortably. They don't deceive you with thrills and trick endings. They don't surprise you with the unforeseen. They are as familiar as the house you live in. Or the smell of your lover's skin. You know how they end, yet you listen as though you don't. In the way that although you know that one day you will die, you live as though you won't. In the Great Stories you know who lives, who dies, who finds love, who doesn't. And yet you want to know again.

—Arundhati Roy, *The God of Small Things*

ONE
MORE
MOUNTAIN
TO CLIMB

rossing the Jordan River proved to be rather disappointing. While it is true that we were crossing the wrong way—from west to east—it still could not escape us that the mighty River Jordan was a trickle, a sluggish, brackish stream overgrown by weeds on either side of its banks. But for the coils of barbed wire and the machine guns, we might have crossed over with a running jump. As it was, we waited hours while papers were checked and then rechecked. Did they worry a bomb would explode over the river and reduce it to the trickle it already was? I am naive about these things, but it struck me more than once during my first passage over the

Jordan that things were being kept deliberately slow more from a sense of history than from a need for security. If they were really worried, they would have made us get off the bus and searched us.

Needless to say, the bus rumbling over the tiny bridge was anticlimactic after the long delay, especially with the foreknowledge that the so-called security check would be repeated once we got to the Jordanian side of the river. There we changed money and had our visas inspected. It was not clear whether we were supposed to offer bribes, though on our return trip our driver-guide assured us that it was de rigueur. Only now does it dawn on me that he pocketed the dirham. Most daunting in our crossing of the Jordan was the scrap of paper, torn off raggedly from a pad, that the immigration official stamped with a rubber stamp. The resultant four lines of Arabic were duly initialed, and the official repeated in English, French, German, Hebrew, and Arabic: "This paper is very important. You will need it to exit Jordan. Keep it carefully. It is very important." To this day I keep that torn scrap in my passport. No one has ever asked to look at it since the moment it was given to me. It is somewhat reassuring that the Muslim and Christian Arabs of the Hashemite Kingdom of Jordan share the same sense of moment about Jordan River crossings as Israeli Jews.

Still, I was disappointed. We had left Jerusalem early in the morning after settling our hotel bill. When the tour bus picked us up for our requisite visit to Jordan, I had expectations of a journey into Jewish (and, therefore, also Christian and Muslim) history. I would be crossing over into the Land of Moab where Ruth and Naomi had roamed, where the Israelites massed before their famous entry into the Holy Land. I would see the ancient city of Petra, not as old as the Hebrew Bible, but Nabatean, and neat, having been featured in an Indiana Jones movie. I would visit Amman, ancient Rabbah Ammon, which *was* a biblical city and now a thriving metropolis, testimony to King Hussein's plans for the modernization of his country.

We had planned to visit Jerash, the archaeological site of ancient Gerasa, a city of the Decapolis, dating back to New Testament times. And, of course, we would visit Madeba, a Muslim village with a thriving church in the middle of town. In the middle of the church, a mosaic floor is roped off. The mosaic contains a map of the ancient world, the oldest map we have of the Holy Land. As it happened, the map proved the key to my understanding of yet another site, one that wasn't part of the package tour at all, but which we added on through a "private arrangement" with our driver.

The previous Saturday afternoon, lingering over Sabbath luncheon under the lemon tree in the courtyard of friends, we drank wine and spoke of our forthcoming trip to Jordan. My hosts were old Israel hands, inveterate travelers. They had been to Jordan already.

"Go to Mount Nebo," Yocheved instructed. I should point out that Yocheved is her Hebrew name; professionally she uses her English name. But her friends call her Yocheved—the same as Moses' mother.

"Nebo isn't on the tour," I truculently told her. I'm a somewhat fussy traveler, I don't like changing hard-planned itineraries, especially in countries where I do not speak the language.

"Go," she insisted, "you won't regret it."

Now, I knew that there were ancient mosaics aplenty on the floors of the churches scattered across the mountain, but I also knew that I would have a surfeit of ancient mosaics in Jordan. So I ventured, still trying to protect my precious vacation plan, as though it were infallible, "I don't know. I think we'll have our fill of churches and mosaics by then."

Yocheved's frustration with me was evident, "Then go for the nostalgia, schmuck!"

Eventually, even I know when to listen to the voice of wisdom, so we made our pilgrimage to Mount Nebo. In our driver's boatlike sixties Chevy, we rattled up the road. The words of the Band's song were rumbling through my brain like a mantra, "I'd stand on the rock where Moses stood . . ." But I was entirely unprepared for what I saw atop Mount Nebo.

Facing west, with the morning sun at our back, standing on that mountain, we could see the River Jordan. From atop Nebo it looked lush, "chilly and wide," as in the song. To the left, south, the Dead Sea. Ahead to the right a bit, Jericho—the city of palms. And past that ancient city and those two famous bodies of water, onward to the very horizon, there lay Israel, Palestine, Canaan, call it what you may—the Promised Land. "Milk and honey on the other side. Hallelujah."

Standing atop Mount Nebo, the nostalgia was overwhelming. Looking out to the Promised Land I was able to imagine it through Moses' eyes. After a forty-year journey in the desert, after a previous forty years as a shepherd, after forty early years as a youth growing up in Pharaoh's court—now, at 120 years of age, the prize he sought was in sight, he could almost reach out and touch it. The breeze at my back buoyed me as I climbed to the highest point on the promontory, the vision before me as palpable as though I stood beside our teacher, Moses, at that stunning moment which marked the culmination of his life.

From Mount Nebo, Moses was able to see the land with the profound knowledge that he himself would never enter it. His eyes also filling with tears as he, too, succumbs to nostalgia, bereft of his lifelong goal—it is too easy to imagine Moses curling up and dying with the Promised Land in sight. Could there be a sadder place on earth than the top of Mount Nebo?

As the last of the Five Books of Moses, Deuteronomy, tells it:

> God spoke to Moses on that very day saying, Ascend this Mountain of transition, Mount Nebo in the land of Moab, facing Jericho, and behold the land of Canaan that I give to the children of Israel to inhabit. And die upon that mountain which you will ascend, be gathered to your ancestors, just as your brother Aaron did on Mount Hor when he was gathered to his ancestors. For you broke faith with Me in the midst of the children of Israel, at the waters of Meribat-Kodesh in the Sinai wilderness. . . . You may view the land from afar, but you may not go there to the land which I give to the children of Israel.

What pathos is contained within these lines. Is it any wonder that Moses dies? After that long journey, to see the land but not get to enter? For the trifling sin of hitting rather than speaking to a rock to get water for the thirsty Israelites? This is Moses, after all, not just any man. He was no schnook, but the very man who *led* the children of Israel. It was he who stood up to Pharaoh, he who ascended Sinai to receive the Ten Commandments, he who took the Jews while they kvetched incessantly and led them through the wilderness to the very door of the Promised Land.

A medieval midrash (a term we'll discuss more fully later in this chapter), commenting on this passage, has Moses say, "These hands which received the Torah are now to wither in the grave?!" According to this midrash, Moses cannot believe he will not reach his goal. He asks God: "Was it for naught that I worked like a horse on behalf of your children?"

Moses is not only bargaining with God here for an extension on life, he is urgently trying to reach his goal: the Promised Land. He can see it before him, shimmering there in the distance. Alas, too much like another desert mirage, it is a goal that will evaporate before his eyes. He'll die just before entering the land. Though he has worked his entire life to reach the territory of his forebears, though he wrought miracles and crossed the Reed Sea, he will not cross the Jordan and enter the sacred territory before him. Though he had mapped out the journey and can clearly see his goal, Moses will not arrive.

For a boy who grew up in the most urbane luxury the world had ever seen, eighty years in the desert—forty with but sheep as his companions, followed by forty with a bunch of carping, ever complaining, runaway slaves—was not the lifestyle he'd been raised to expect for himself. And now, at the end of the long, long road, there was still one more mountain for Moses to climb. He was tired, more tired than he'd been at any time in his long, full life. He was determined not to let the weariness show as he trudged to the top of the mountain to fulfill God's last, most cruel commands. Appearances matter, so he kept up the good facade. But how disheartening could it be that on his 120th birthday God set him the task of climbing Mount Nebo? The mountain was bad, but not unscalable—let's face it: Nebo is no Everest. Still, how could Moses find the strength to climb when he knew that at the summit it was his task to see the Promised Land that he would never enter? Where did Moses find the will to obey God and climb the mountain when his duty at the top of the peak was to die?

Before he ever started his journey to the summit Moses knew his fate. He had come to the end of the road. As Deuteronomy elsewhere has it, he faced death, much as he faced life, with vigor, his "sap unabated." Could any of us have the courage of Moses, to knowingly come to the end of the journey with the end in sight, yet just out of reach? How could his eyes but cloud with tears as he turned west to see the Holy Land and faced the failure of his arrival there? Atop Mount Nebo, Moses had to reckon his life. He had struck an Egyptian down and killed him. He struck a rock and failed to give glory to God, even as he gave precious water to the people Israel. He climbed Mount Sinai to receive the Torah, yet descended to find his flock frenzied in their worship of the Golden Calf. He climbed once more to receive the second tablets of the Law, only to be overwhelmed at the immensity of their demand and enforcement. Now he trudged slowly up Mount Nebo, his mind racing. Standing on the very summit, Moses faced death alone.

A bit farther to the east of Mount Nebo and a few miles south, one comes to the town of Madeba. In the heart of the church there is a mosaic floor—one that dates back to the fifth century and contains a map of the world, carefully laid out in its tiles, still brilliant after fifteen centuries. The Madeba map is a map of the spirit, for at its center is the Holy Land and at *its* center is, of course, Jerusalem. There in Madeba, Jordan, east of the Jordan River, east of Mount Nebo, a map orients its readers to look west to Jerusalem.

Jewish custom dictates that prayers are to be recited facing east, and the medieval Spanish poet Yehuda ha-Levi captures the sentiment in two Hebrew words, *libi bamizrah,* my heart is in the east. Of old we are instructed that the journey to the spirit is the journey to the east. Yet if one wants to see the Promised Land from atop Mount Nebo, one must face west, in quite the opposite direction. The ancient Madeba map held fair warning that it may not always be clear which way one should be looking to gain a sense of direction.

Moses realized that no matter which way he faced, he faced death. But how he faced it, what he looked forward to and what he looked back upon, these were the keys to his redemption. A ninth-century midrash builds on the biblical detail that Moses' generation, the generation that left Egypt in the Exodus and wandered the Sinai desert for forty years, was condemned to die there and not enter the Promised Land any more than Moses would. The midrash expands the biblical narrative with a macabre twist in the story. We are told that every evening, when the encampment reached their destination for that day's journey, the tribes would set up camp and each

Israelite would dig his own grave. As night fell, one by one, the children of Israel would lay themselves down into the desert earth for what might be a night's rest or eternal rest.

Each morning, the legend goes, most of the Israelites would arise to face the new dawn afresh. But some remained in their graves, there to be covered by their loved ones, mourned briefly, and left behind in the wilderness. Only when the last of that generation of slaves who had built the Golden Calf had died out could the tribes cross the Jordan east to west and enter the Promised Land of Israel.

Here's the question of perspective: What did they see as they lay in their graves each night wondering whether they would rise to see the next day? Did they myopically notice the walls of earth surrounding them, closing in on them? Or did they look outward, past the barriers of their mortality to see the stars, the very heavens spread like a tent above them? And what did they think on the morrow? Woe is me, for tonight it may be my turn to die? Or did they give thanks for their life and breath, perhaps even rejoice that with the passing of the old comes the new; so that on that day when all Israel rose from their graves they would enter the Promised Land a new generation, freed from the shackles of slavery at last and ready to conquer the land God gave them.

The lesson of this thousand-year-old midrash seems to be: In the grave lies redemption. In the Promised Land lies redemption. Yet can redemption also be found in the wanderings in the wilderness? Could the Israelites orient themselves to redemption? Could Moses? Did Moses imagine his life a failure or a success when he stood at Mount Nebo? Did he, as I did, succumb to nostalgia, or was his perspective keener, more positive, a vision for us to follow?

Was Moses able to find the right direction to affect his own redemption? As we remember it, he redeemed the Jews from bondage. But is that how he saw it? Which way did Moses face as he contemplated his long, long life? Which way will any of us face as we do the same, whether midway through life's journey or near the road's end. Of course, we have no way of knowing exactly where we are on the road, we could get run over by a car tomorrow or travel on for many years to come. We do not have a life map with an arrow pointing "You Are Here." So we have to learn, as Moses did on Nebo (and for many years before that, too), how to orient ourselves.

How to travel on the road of life and be sure that it is the road to redemption.

This is a study book. It is, in fact, a book about a book. The Book. In the pages that follow we will study the Bible, particularly the first half of the book called Exodus. There we can find the narrative of the life of Moses. How he was born, raised, fled Egypt, returned there, and then led the Jews forth. We will read the story together, travel together with the Israelites to the very foot of Mount Sinai. What we will learn reading the story of the road to redemption will help each of us find redemption in our own lives. We will read how a people went from slavery to freedom, from tyranny to covenant, from chaos to law. We will read how individuals find themselves in communities and how communities form a nation. The story of Exodus speaks of community formation and the growth of its leadership.

It is a story that still speaks, if we read and study with a listening ear. We may learn from a very old Book how we can move forward with a relationship to God, to history, and to community. By careful reading of Exodus we may learn the lessons necessary to enter the Promised Land. Like Moses and the Israelites, we can gain the insight to orient our lives, to see forward and back, and to look upward to the stars.

In order to read together, I should be explicit about *how* we will be reading. Since every act of reading is itself an orientation—both to the text we encounter and to the life we live—we bring our lives to the page as we read. This is true no matter who we are; it makes little difference whether we are reading Shakespeare or the *New York Times,* a poem or a recipe. The encounter between our reading selves and the printed word is an active one. We climb the mountain; we walk the road. We cannot be passive as readers, no matter how cozily we may be curled in a chair or how we grip our book as the subway car rocks back and forth. The words we read change us, just as who we are affects how we understand the very letters on the page. Every act of reading is midrash, an interpretation, a searching out of meaning.

How much more so when the book we read is the Bible. In reading Scripture, we enter the congregation of readers who have come before us. It is a large congregation—more, far more than the original

600,000 who received the Book at Sinai. It does not make a difference if you believe that the Torah was given to Moses at Sinai, it is not a prerequisite for Bible reading. Nor is it a prerequisite for studying with this book.

In fact, I write without regard as to whether the readers of *this* book are "believers" of that Book. Allow me to explain. For those who are churched (or synagogued, if you will), reading the Bible often follows a prescribed set of assumptions and beliefs. The very encounter between you and Scripture is mediated through a particular set of community reading habits. Thus, if you are a Methodist, you will read somewhat differently than if you are a Baptist. If you are a Lubovitch Chasid, you will read differently than if you are a Reform Jew. If you are evangelical, you will read differently than if you are liberal Protestant. If you are Catholic, different again. If you are Muslim, you won't even be reading the same book, but you may be reading some of the same stories.

Now, if you are reading this book, you may be interested in reading "outside your church," as it were. This may be due to intellectual curiosity. It may be due to a crisis in faith. It may be that you are reading this book because you believe the Bible to be an interesting artifact of Western culture and somewhat worth your time. It may be that you saw a cartoon about Moses and want to get to the bottom of it, the real story. Or, you may be piously reading this book in a synagogue or church study group. The point of this book is to guide you in your encounter with the biblical narrative, to open Exodus for reading in a variety of ways.

I have been engaged in public reading of Scripture for a long time. So let me give "full disclosure" here and tell you what I think I am up to in the various readings of the Exodus and Moses story I offer in this volume. I intend to come at the stories primarily from two angles, in the hope that more than one set of perspectives will give us a better view of the story. I think the story of redemption is still important today. I think that a modern take on the story is needed to enable us to enter into a dialogue with the Moses narrative at all. I also think we have a lot to learn from how our forebears read the story in centuries past. So I will try both.

The modern strategies of reading tend to the literary, sociological, psychological, and, frankly, secular or unreligious. Literary because the story of Exodus and the redemption of Israel is, above all, story: a magnificent piece of Western literature. Sociological because it is a story about community formation, how groups work, fail, and ultimately come to be in contractual or covenantal relationship. Psychological because it is also the story of one leader, the intensely personal story of Moses, with whom we are able to identify strongly as a result of this type of reading. Finally, my approach is secular because I believe the story is powerful enough, wise enough to teach everyone, regardless of whether they hold religious beliefs. I think Exodus speaks profoundly to our late-twentieth-century condition. I believe that through the study of the Israelites' journey to community we will all learn valuable lessons about our own place in community, and the importance of growing our communities into a proud nation. In short, I think the story of Exodus already informs the "American dream," but I also think it still has a great deal to teach us as we struggle to keep that dream vibrant.

The ancient readings I will offer come from an amorphous collection of Scriptural meditations called midrash. This searching out of Scripture was done by rabbis over a millennium and more, from the late first century until well into the twelfth century. Some people reckon that midrash is still being written even in our twentieth century. For people who value the Bible, it often cries out for interpretation. Laconic language begs to be expanded. Midrash is the act of reading between the lines, inferring what the Bible's characters meant to say or should have said. Often, the process of midrash brings the ethics and social norms of the time of the midrash writer back into the biblical narrative. The ancient rabbis excelled in teasing new meanings out of the Bible, and their imaginative rereadings have been collected in dozens upon dozens of volumes in Hebrew and Aramaic.

I will quote and translate texts here from the broad range of midrash because I believe that the rabbis of old were careful readers who invested a great deal in making the Bible speak to each generation of readers. I, too, am a rabbi and am most comfortable reading and teaching from my own particular tradition. But I believe that *each* tradition has a great deal to teach us, whether Jewish, Christian, Muslim, or of another religion not "of the Book," or of secular humanist traditions. The greatest works of Western literature are often meditations on the Bible.

So, I write as a rabbi and as a Jew, but I invite all readers to share in this study of Exodus, for I believe it is a story that speaks to us all. It is no accident that Afro-Americans resonate with the story of freedom from bondage. It is no coincidence that Muslims include Moses among the prophets of their tradition. It is not for naught that Christianity focuses again and again on the liberation from Egypt, and that liberation and redemption is an essential part of virtually all Christian theology, ancient and modern. The story we are about to study can still speak to us and teach us today.

We began by considering Moses, standing on Mount Nebo, looking out to the Holy Land at the very end of his life. But the story of Exodus begins with the birth of Moses and with his big sister standing at the banks of the Nile looking out to see what would become of him, a baby adrift in a basket.

THE
BABY
IN THE
BASKET

revity is a virtue, often a necessity. This is particularly true when spinning biography, whether of oneself or of others. I recall an idyllic sabbatical year I spent nervously playing the Cambridge don. There, over tea or sherry, one was called upon to explicate a life in the space of a swallow. One notably trying biographical inquisition took place for me at my first high-table in one of the old schools—Gonville and Caius.

High-table has its forms and procedures, made all the more dear to dons who earn very little salary but revel in the all-you-can-eat atmosphere of fine dining, and even finer drinking during the elaborate ritual. The faculty table actually is high, raised on a dais, half a foot off the floor, towering above the mere mortal Cambridge undergraduates. Dons and students alike dined in academic gowns, but the dons ate haute cuisine while the students ate undergraduate swill.

There I was, a guest at a six-hundred-year-old college, the new boy on the block, an awestruck rabbi from America, come to see how civilization is played out at its best. I was seated, according to custom, to the left of the Master of House, in this case a retired Scottish professor who had made his reputation interrogating guests on occasions just like this. We began with my biography—a skill I had apparently not yet learned, for I began with the wrong answer.

"Just what is it you do?" inquired the don. I'm afraid I waxed expansive, having mistaken his empty query for actual interest. I went on and on about being American (as though that were not eminently clear to these Cambridge birds the moment I opened my mouth), about being a rabbi as well as an academic, about doing research in Cambridge with Hebrew manuscripts yet at the same time studying the works of the Church fathers in the hope of doing a comparative study between them and my rabbis of the first through sixth centuries.

"Well," the Scottish professor burred, with a brogue thick enough to cut with the very old, very heavy silver service set at high-table, "I think this may be the very first time in our six-hundred-plus years history here at Caius that we've actually had a *rabbi* at our table."

I confess I did not know what to make of his pronouncement, delivered with just enough hint of a sneer to make me wonder whether I was not experiencing a touch of genteel anti-Semitism at high-table. I remained silent, nervous and unsure of what to respond. The Master continued, "A rabbi, a rabbi, I rather had expected that a rabbi would be someone more venerable."

"Please," I chirped without thinking, "feel free to venerate me."

When laughter broke out down the entire length of high-table I realized that this inquisition was ritual hazing, and that my inadvertently snappy response had won me a place at the table and in the hearts of the dons of Gonville and Caius. Later, when we retired to the Senior Commons Room for port and cigars, I took aside my host, a British Jew who was a member of Caius. I asked him how I should respond when subjected to such an inquiry in the future.

"Oh," he replied, "we always look for the short answer of what it is one does, much like your American 'sound bite.' So, when asked, I myself reply History." Indeed, I had learned my lesson. Nevertheless, it took the entire year at Cambridge for me to be able to respond with any semblance of a straight face when asked what is it I do. In America I might well properly say Judaica or Religion or Theology. But at Cambridge the correct answer was the reply, "I do Divinity."

The laconic brevity of this biography finds a far more estimable ancestor in the biblical description of Moses, often referred to as "our venerable rabbi." When Moses did Divinity, he did DIVINITY, having spoken face-to-face with God. Yet the Bible's introduction to this towering figure of religious history is a model of brevity. No annunciation scenes, no fanfares, just a sound bite worthy of Cambridge high-table.

> Pharaoh commanded all his people, saying: Every Jewish boy who is born shall be thrown into the River Nile, while every Jewish girl shall be kept alive. A man of the tribe of Levi went and took a daughter of Levi. The woman became pregnant and gave birth to a son; when she saw that he was good, she hid him for three months. When she could no longer hide him, she took a reed basket for him and daubed it with pitch and bitumen. She placed the boy in the basket and put it in the reeds at the bank of the River Nile. His sister stood watch from afar that she might know what would be done to him. . . . (Exod. 1:22–2:4)

In a mere five verses an entire life is set in motion, a life that begins at the banks of the River Nile and ends atop Mount Nebo, overlooking the River Jordan—for the baby in the basket will grow up to lead the Jews out of slavery in Egypt, and he will bring them to covenantal freedom in the Promised Land. The brevity of the telling is typical of the Bible's laconic nature. The eponymous hero of the Torah, the very man for whom the Five Books are named, is given his biography in the space of but four verses, after the scene is set. Against a backdrop of "the slaughter of the innocents," baby Moses is set afloat in an ark, wholly under the direction of the currents of the Nile, yet guided invisibly by the gentle hand of God. The pathos of the family scene is neatly etched, a loving mother vainly trying to hide her good boy. After all seems lost, his sister cannot tear her eyes away from her little brother. She tries her best to see into the future to learn what will become of him.

Telling the story now, half a century after the Nazi slaughter of the innocents, still brings a chill to those who can as readily imagine the separations of families, the good children set afloat, too often to drown, in the tide of Aryan chauvinism. The baby in the basket could as easily be Anne Frank, or any other of the thousands and myriads of Jewish children sacrificed in the course of Jewish history. It is equally appropriate for other religious readers of the Bible to see themselves in this brief biography: the slaughtered Armenians, the Muslims of Serbo-Croatia, the African slaves who identify so wholly with these martyred children of Israel. For more than two thousand years this story has resonated among readers, whether as the very Gospel tale or as midrash, a rereading of the narrative so that it speaks not of Moses but of the reader in his or her own community and time.

Of course, when the rabbis of old, those spinners of midrash, themselves read the story of baby Moses, they felt no need to allegorize the tale as though it spoke of them—it *did* speak of them, it was their history as well as their sacred story, for Moses son of Amram was their revered ancestor, their Rabbi Moses, their very flesh and blood. As Torah, the sacred Scripture's very brevity nevertheless cried out to the rabbis to do midrash and fill in the Semitic minimalism with Hellenistic detail and depth. So, when the midrash treats this brief tale, it characteristically seizes on a peculiarity of the narrative to make its point. When the rabbis read the tale slowly, as they were wont to do, they puzzled over an anomaly in the brief narrative, a bump in the road from Egypt to the Holy Land.

We are introduced to the story of Moses with a family sketch: man from tribe of Levi marries woman from same. Have baby. Set him afloat after three months. The bare-bones nature of this story could qualify it for mere jottings in a cub reporter's notebook. I imagine the ire of the editor who then turns to the next fact, as yet unrevealed: The baby has an older sister! How can this be? Did we not establish that man marries woman and has baby, with no mention of previous children, older siblings, girls who worry about their little brothers. There was no narration of other marriages, half-siblings, concubines, any of the narrative devices that spiced the family plot in Genesis. Where did this older sister come from? Our cub reporter may have some follow-up calls to make before this story is set in hot lead.

It is, of course, precisely these kinds of gaps that make the biblical narrative famous for its brevity. In presenting the introductory biography of Moses as sound bite, holes that want filling appear in the biblical story. The rabbis of the ancient midrash gladly oblige. As they fill in the gaps, retelling the story in their own image, they shift the focus of the narrative away from the savior of Israel and onto the problems that beset families across the millennia. Let us listen to their retelling of Moses' family history leading up to his birth.

> Pharaoh commanded all his people, saying: "Every Jewish boy who is born shall be thrown into the River Nile, while every Jewish girl shall be kept alive." When Amram, who was a leader of the tribe of Levi, heard Pharaoh's decree, he was deeply concerned. What avail would it be to have children if the boys were to be drowned? His concern turned to depression as he felt impotent against Pharaoh's evil decree. So, summoning his courage, he called his children, Aaron and Miriam, and before them told his wife, Yocheved, that they could no longer live as husband and wife. If they could not raise sons but only bear them to their deaths, what point was there being married? And so, a sorrowful Amram divorced his wife and the other men of the tribe of Levi soon followed suit.
>
> Miriam was six years old at the time, yet she already had the gift of prophecy. She foresaw that her mother would bear one more son to Amram, and this son, not yet born, would be the redeemer of the Jews. It would be he who would end the massacre of the innocents, it would be he who would lead the Jews out of slavery and to freedom.
>
> So little Miriam told her prophecy to her father and urged him to remarry her desolate mother. "Father," she cajoled him, "evil Pharaoh has decreed only against the boys while you wish to uproot everything!" Amram heeded her words and "A man of the tribe of Levi went and took a daughter of Levi. The woman became pregnant and gave birth to a son; when she saw that he was good, she hid him for three months. When she could no longer hide him, she took a reed basket for him and daubed it with pitch and bitumen. She placed the

boy in the basket and put it in the reeds at the bank of the River Nile."
At this point an enraged Amram, having his worst fears confirmed,
smacked his daughter on the head and shouted at her, "What has
become of your stupid prophecy now?" Thus Miriam watched to see
if her prophecy would come true: "His sister stood watch from afar
that she might know what would be done to him. . . ."

Note well that this baroque retelling of the story in Exodus pre-
serves the words of Scripture virtually verbatim. It merely resets
them in a different context. The midrash also takes a line of the
Passover Haggadah, the very ritual still recited in Jewish homes to
celebrate the Exodus, and places it ("evil Pharaoh has decreed . . ."),
along with Scripture, in Miriam's tender yet prophetic mouth, again
changing the context of the original. In midrashic retelling, the rabbis use the bricks of Scripture and rabbinic tradition to build a different edifice, one that is apposite for their own day and age.

This ancient midrash is not without its echoes in our own time.
We hear of a family that undergoes a trial separation during
extreme outside stress on the marriage. We see a child of the first
marriage eager to fulfill her dream of seeing her parents back
together and the family restored. There is a father who reacts vio-
lently to the stress, while his little daughter keeps the faith and an
eye on her baby brother. Each of these themes from an ancient
midrash's retelling of the Bible story still begs for unpacking a millennium and a half after they were first suggested.

Yet before we treat the midrash on Moses' birth as an opportunity
for family therapy, we should note that the underpinnings of the rabbinic retelling of the biblical story serve a broader, more mythic function. While it is true that we can read of Amram and Yocheved's
divorce and remarriage as a paradigm for modern family dynamics,
we must not forget that the stories of Exodus function on two levels.
Yes, there is family, and in the historic makeup of the Israelites, family equals tribe. But there is also the reality that the Israelites are a
tribal confederation. To put it more simply: The story of this family is
also symbolic of the nation at large. What happens to Moses' family is
emblematic of what will happen to the Jewish people.

So, we have to read even the rabbinic version as something larger
than a family narrative. We are called upon to do some midrash on

the midrash. Let us take a few moments and unpack the baggage carried by this rabbinic narrative of a millennium and a half ago. It will help us understand the worldview of the rabbis who told it and at the same time make us see in the Bible story what they saw: a narrative that spoke to the essence of every generation.

I would suggest that the deep structure of the midrash's story goes something like this: The founding family is fractured. Outside stress, persecution, the vicissitudes of history cause rupture in the very body of the people. Inspired leadership brings reconciliation (what the later kabbalists would call *tikkun,* restoration). Yet even then, even with rebirth, there are still hardships to be endured. Some will lose faith. Yet others, those who are truly called to leadership, will keep the faith and look to the future. Even though there will be hardship to endure, that vision leads to ultimate redemption.

Stated thus, the rabbinic retelling of the birth of Moses as the story of a divorced family offers a mythic paradigm, a model of national redemption and hope. The midrash helps us see the motifs of the entire book of Exodus—indeed, the motifs of the entire Judeo-Christian worldview—played out in the theater of Moses' family. This makes us appreciate the rabbis of old as acute readers, keenly sensitive to literary composition as they retell the story in their own idiom. They also have a sense of moment, not without a tinge of irony. The moment is as much ours as theirs. Leave it to clever readers fifteen hundred years ago to provide a biography for their leader that will include a "broken home." According to this reading, Moses is a child who wound up in foster care and still made good! It sounds like a plot for a late-twentieth-century (or a late-nineteenth-century) novel.

The irony is twofold. First, this plot undermines itself. For if the new improved story of Moses' birth is the story of a boy from a bad neighborhood, an underprivileged child from a dysfunctional home who has "made it" under the care of his new patrician parentage, he achieves greatness only when he brings down the very family and culture that raised him and returns to his humble origins and birth siblings. The strong African woman (Miriam) assures his placement and parentage, even as she herself prays and hopes for liberation. This, too, has a late-twentieth-century ring to the plot. Again, the rabbis in their tale-spinning have caught the gist of the story.

Though the divorce and remarriage motif is far afield from the biblical plot of Exodus, the point of Exodus is neatly captured by this tale. It reaches resolution only when the tyrant Pharaoh, the persecutor of the innocents, in his hubris, unwittingly harbors the hero who will destroy him.

The second irony is this: Every family going through the throes of divorce imagines the conflict somewhat mythically. For the children involved, divorce is no mere disruption of the family, it is rupture on a cosmic scale. For the battling spouses it is not merely sniping, it is global warfare. One spouse plays the tyrant to the other's enslaved victim. Reconciliation may lead to further disruption and disaster. If the family of the midrash is meant to be metaphor for the fate of God's chosen people Israel, then the separation of Israel from Egypt in the biblical story conversely serves as metaphor for the dissolution of a marriage.

We've gotten ahead of ourselves in the Exodus narrative, and I fear I've presumed too much of the plot in my hurry to unpack a wonderfully baroque midrash that explicates a hiccup in the Bible story. For while I am interested in the methods by which the ancients and we moderns can wrest meaning out of the Bible's story—and while we're at it, our lives—I do not wish to lose sight of the biblical narrative itself. So let us return to reconsider the Book of Exodus' introduction to our hero. In fact, if you turned to your own Bible, you will already have found that the story of Moses which I quote is not the very beginning of the book.

My last sentence demands an aside about "your own Bible." This book, *The Road to Redemption,* is a book that studies the biblical Book of Exodus. To do so, I translate portions of Exodus from the original Hebrew into English in order to discuss them. Be warned, what I offer is not all of the Book of Exodus, it is not my intention to provide a Bible translation but rather a study book for the story. Further, not everyone will agree with my translation. Rendering an ancient language (approximately twenty-five hundred to three thousand years old) into modern English idiom is hard enough. Translating the cultures of Egypt, the Levant, and Mesopotamia to North America is even harder. So, do not rely on me alone. Get another translation to compare mine with, even two. That way you can compare texts and, as it were, triangulate toward the original

Hebrew. Use a denominational translation and then another. Since all translations are somewhat denominational, I would recommend using a Jewish translation and a Christian translation. You are not required to learn Hebrew to read this book. But you probably should have an English Bible at hand while you read it. That way you can learn the basic story, if you do not know it already. And, if you do know it, you will have the opportunity to compare my readings with the biblical narrative, to answer the question: Is that really in the Bible? Perhaps you will be provoked by this book to see things in the Bible you never noticed before.

Indeed, if you look to the Book of Exodus, you will see that twenty-one verses have unfolded before evil Pharaoh ever commands the drowning of babies. Like at high-table, there is the short version and the longer version of every story. It's time for us to backtrack a bit and get some fuller background to the Moses narrative. It is not sufficient to simply say of Moses, "He does divinity."

MIDWIFERY

The Five Books of Moses are exactly that, five separate books, each with its own style and agenda. The fact that in synagogues they are sewn together on an enormous scroll sometimes obscures the differences of the books one from another, even as they share certain common facts, characters, and motifs. From Genesis through Deuteronomy, God remains a central character in the Five Books. The family of Abraham and his grandson Israel remain the covenant-people of choice throughout the Pentateuch (Latin for "five books"). The Promised Land of Canaan, the Land of Israel, is the property of preference and covenantal promise.

But still each book remains distinct. Indeed, anyone who has ever seen a Torah scroll lifted in a synagogue knows how awkwardly huge these five books are when bound together. As a scroll, the Torah (which is the rabbinic Hebrew designation, par excellence, for these five books together) is so unwieldy as to require not one but two staves to be wound upon. In the elegant parlance of the Jewish world, these wooden sticks that form the spine for the parchment-skin rolled around them are called Trees of Life.

But even before the advent of bound printed books, it was common in antiquity for each biblical book to be presented separately as well as bound together in the synagogue. Each rolled around its own Tree of Life, the Five Books were preserved in their separate forms for study, if not liturgical usage. Each scroll thus resembled the myriads of other books of the Greek and then Roman world. And like those works as well, the separate scrolls lacked an outer spine upon which the title could be printed. So the works, in Hebrew, came to be named after the opening words of each book—not necessarily with any indication of their contents—because one could always fold back the beginning of a scroll and peek at how it began.

Genesis (as it is titled in Latin) was called in Hebrew *beresheit,* after the initial word, "In the Beginning," or, more accurately, "When [God] began." The third book of the Torah, Leviticus (accurately titled in Latin; for the contents refer to the laws of the tribe of Levi, the priests), in Hebrew is simply *vayikra,* "called," for its opening words, "The Lord called to Moses." Ironically, the fourth of the Books has a more accurate Hebrew title than its Latin description. In the latter it is called Numbers, presumably because of the repeated listings of the tribes and their census. Yet in Hebrew it is called, again after one of its initial words, *bamidbar,* "in the wilderness," which succinctly captures the locale and flavor of the work. The final book of the Torah, Deuteronomy, has the Hebrew name *devarim* or "things," which is not very descriptive at all. This is because the first verse of that book begins, "These are the things which Moses said . . ." Again, the Latin designation of Deuteronomy more accurately refers to the "repetition of the Law," which is the work's content.

I've skipped the second book until now, for since it is the one unrolled, as it were, before us, I wanted to treat it separately. We know that it is called Exodus, which certainly hits the nail on the head for content. But in Hebrew, drawing on the *incipit* (Latin for initial words), it is called, simply, *shemot,* the Hebrew for "Names." The book opens with a list of "the names of the sons of Israel who came to Egypt, with Jacob each came with his family." This simple opening continues through four verses, listing each of the sons of Jacob, eleven in number. Verse five continues, "The total of souls who were Jacob's offspring were seventy, for Joseph was already in Egypt."

As in the story that introduces Moses, Exodus is a marvel of minimalism, stunningly succinct. With no more than a list of eleven names, adding Jacob-Israel's to round out an even dozen, the four opening verses of Exodus invoke fully half of the previous book, Genesis. Now Genesis has fifty chapters taken up variously with such things as the creation of the universe, Noah's flood, and the call by God of Abraham. At the end of the twenty-fifth chapter we first meet Jacob, and from then on he and his offspring assume center stage. Here, too, Genesis is neatly divided, for the latter twenty-five chapters fall into two halves. The first half is the story of Jacob: his cheating of his brother Esau; his deception of his father, Isaac; his flight; his marriage to four wives and fathering of twelve sons, the tribes of Israel. All in all, Genesis might be characterized as a book of sex and violence. If it were not Holy Scripture, it could be considered a potboiler or soap opera. It is a work that focuses on the individual and on the dysfunction of the family. From Abraham and his wife, Sarah, through Jacob and his sons, in particular, the narrative charts a tormented family. The grand irony of Genesis is that as members of the family reach relationship with God, the family structure itself breaks down. It is only in the end, when Joseph appears on the scene, that the family finds reconciliation with both God and one another. From chapter thirty-seven to the end of the book of Genesis, Jacob's favorite son, Joseph, commands the spotlight.

We read of Joseph's arrogance, his brothers' perfidy, which results in his sale as an Egyptian slave, and his rise to power in Egypt until he stands as second in command to Pharaoh. Joseph as steward of Egypt saves them from seven years of famine through his foresight, a grace of God. Joseph forgives his brothers when they come to

Egypt searching for food. Then, after many long years, Joseph reunites with his beloved father, Jacob, when the sons of Jacob-Israel come to sojourn in Egypt under Joseph's protection. The book of Genesis ends with Joseph, savior of his family and savior of the people of Egypt, embalmed in his casket, resting from his heroic labors as viceroy of the pharaonic court. Joseph, a Jewish foreigner, risen to power like a young Henry Kissinger, lies dead, securely entombed. And Genesis draws to a close with a happy ending, the family of Israel secure in Egypt with food aplenty and the memory of their powerful ancestor Joseph a talisman of protection.

All this is invoked in the first four verses of the next book of the Torah, Exodus, and then in the fifth verse, which elevates Joseph above his brothers as the sustainer in Egypt he surely was to them. And then a sixth verse catches us up to the action at the end of Genesis and moves us onward into the new book, "So Joseph died, and all his brethren, and all of that generation." The seventh verse expansively lets us see the intervening years under the protection of Joseph's memory, "The children of Israel were fruitful, they swarmed, they multiplied and grew strong exceedingly, until the land was full of them."

This marks the difference between Genesis and Exodus. For if Genesis is a book of the individual within a family, Exodus is a book of tribes within a nation. The story of the freed slaves who come into covenant with God at Mount Sinai is a far cry from the sex and violence of the earlier book of the Torah. Yes, there will be violence in Exodus as the slaves are freed from the oppressive slavery of Egypt, but it is the violence of God against an evil tyrant. If there is bickering in Exodus, it is not the bickering that takes place in an unhappy family but the struggle of slaves to become a free people and to recognize that such freedom carries responsibility and commitment.

The shift from the themes of Genesis to those very different themes of Exodus having been heralded in the first six verses, the story can now unfold apace. The seventh verse of Exodus is subtle, for even as we read of the successes of Israel's offspring, of their phenomenal growth and beginnings as a nation, a seed of worry is planted. Not only are we warned that "the land was full of them," making clear the potential possibility of indigenous Egyptians feeling threatened, but

we are even given a glimpse of how the Egyptians viewed the
Israelites. A string of verbs is employed: "they were fruitful, they
swarmed, they multiplied, they grew strong." These verbs are modi-
fied: "Exceedingly." But most telling is that verb, buried in the chain,
"they swarmed." It is a verb used in the creation story of Genesis to
denote the swarms of lower creatures who emerge from the watery
depths.

With that one word—swarm—we hear the minor chord, the note
that tells us that all will not be well as Exodus progresses. The Egyptians view these Jews like vermin, swarming everywhere, the land
full of them. We can hear the cadences of bias, anti-Semitism, racism
in every century. One imagines the Egyptians complaining about
those damn Israelites, "They're shiftless, lazy, the men don't work
and the women have more babies to get more welfare. They're clan-
nish, they are not like us, they are the Other." There is more here
than the snobbism of "Not Our Zip Code, Dear"; this is full-blown
hatred brewing—first for the successes of these pushy Jews, next for
their ubiquity and apparent upward mobility; in the end, something
must be done. There needs to be a final solution to this problem.

Alas, the next seven verses of Exodus set the theme for the book:
no longer the successes of Joseph, but the enslavement of the Jews.

> A new king rose over Egypt who knew not Joseph. He said to his
> people, "Behold, this people, the Israelites are more plentiful and
> mightier than we. We must deal shrewdly with them, lest they
> continue to grow. For then, if we may go to war they might join
> with our enemies and war against us and ascend from the land."
>
> So they set taskmasters upon them in order to afflict them with
> their burdens. They built garrison cities for Pharaoh: Pithom and
> Ramses. The more they afflicted them the more they grew and
> spread, so that they dreaded the Israelites. So Egypt enslaved the
> Israelites with hard labor. They made their lives bitter with hard
> slavery, mortar and bricks and field slavery; all the hard labors with
> which they enslaved them.

This "new king" is a real piece of work. It is all but inconceivable
that any Egyptian, let alone a royal, could know so little of Egyptian
history that he "knew not Joseph." Indeed, the story of Joseph was

seminal to royal history, for Joseph's plan not only saved the Egyptians from starvation during famine years, but in payment for the food doled out brought all the real property of Egypt under the control of Pharaoh. In other words, Joseph's Pharaoh and all subsequent pharaohs owed Joseph their very fortunes. It was he, the Jew, who made them the landowners they were. It was he, ironically, who buttressed their claims to divinity by giving them the power to go with their blasphemous claims of godhood.

A medieval midrash wryly notes the convenience of this new pharaoh's memory: "That ingrate Pharaoh repudiated Joseph's beneficence! It says in Scripture, he 'knew not Joseph.' Yet even to this very day Egypt knows of the gifts of Joseph. Obviously he knew, he just refused to attend to Joseph's legacy, he repudiated his beneficence. And in the end, that Pharaoh also repudiated the beneficence of the Blessed Holy One, as it is written, '[Pharaoh said to Moses,] "Who is this Lord . . . ?"' (Exod. 5:2)"

This astute observation, made a thousand years ago, incisively points to the power politics of the situation. A cynical leader knows only too well that his power is threatened by too good a memory. For to know history is to know that his power derives from the very people he fears will overcome him. So, as have dictators for millennia since, he demonizes his perceived enemy. First he forgets the good they did his nation, his family, and himself. Next he plots against them. Then he identifies them as a potential enemy. Finally he enslaves them. If it is a truism that the one who forgets history is doomed to repeat it, it seems equally true that the one who brings doom must first make history be forgotten.

The cynicism of this crass power play is reflected upon by another medieval midrash, probably from the ninth century. In commenting on the verse in the opening of the chapter, "So Joseph died, and all his brethren, and all of that generation," it cites a much earlier rabbinic adage: "Hate power." It is no wonder that an oppressed people, almost a millennium exiled from their land, should have no truck with power. But this advice is internalized: Do not only hate the powers that be, hate all power, even your own. How does it apply to Joseph? The midrash continues: "For power buries all who wield it . . . for Joseph was among the youngest of Jacob's offspring, yet died before the others. Power buries all who wield it."

This profound mistrust of power is wedded in the rabbinic mind to the hubris of Pharaoh. He cannot acknowledge the human sources of his power, especially as he pretends to godhood. How much more so will Pharaoh deny the truest source of power, the King of the King of Kings, the Blessed Holy One? For the rabbis, this is an essential lesson of Exodus. It is a book for all, for God is the God of all, the Creator of the Universe. Thus, God represents all the downtrodden much as the Book of Exodus speaks to all who are weary and wary of power. The Book of Exodus speaks to all who wield power as it warns them not to forget the sources of their power, human and divine. For though a pharaoh may enslave a people, the people will rise, with the help of God, to overthrow the tyrant. It is a hope and promise for the poor and enslaved, "Power buries all who wield it."

Of course, this sermon does not merely derive from these seven verses of Exodus, but it is the message of the book at large. It is a profound and central message of Exodus, one that recognizes God's role as central and profound. It is not the only message of the book, and other themes harmonize in concert with it as the plot progresses. But the universalism of opposing tyranny cannot be ignored for even a moment. It is what gives birth to the redemption that follows enslavement. And, like all birthing, it wants a midwife. And it is just so that the Exodus narrative continues.

> The king of Egypt said to the midwives of the Hebrews—one of whom was named Shifra and the other of whom was named Pu'ah—he said, "When you assist the birthing of the Hebrew women and look to the birthing-stones, if it be a son, kill him! If a daughter, she lives!"
>
> But the midwives feared God, so they did not do as the king of Egypt had directed them. And so, they let [all] the children live.
>
> The king of Egypt summoned the midwives and asked them, "Why did you do this thing, letting the children live?"
>
> The midwives answered Pharaoh, "Not like the Egyptian women are these Hebrew women, they are so animate that before the midwife arrives they have birthed."
>
> God dealt well with the midwives, and the people grew many and were very strong. And because the midwives feared God, God

established households for them. But Pharaoh commanded all his
people, saying, "Every son who is born shall you throw into the
Nile, but every daughter may live."

Let us begin with the murders. Evil Pharaoh commands that the
boys must die. Of course, as with every maniacal leader, we cannot
look for a rational explanation. Everett Fox points out in his commentary to his own felicitous translation of the passage that a rational tyrant would not destroy his own slave workforce. But, like
Hitler, Pharaoh is looking for a final solution, not a labor pool. The
rabbis of old are even more acute readers. They observe three stages
in Pharaoh's descent to murderous madness. First, he commands
the Israelite boys be killed upon the birth stool. When that fails, he
commands that they be drowned. But in the end, his command is to
all his people to kill every son who is born. Here, the rabbis of the
Talmud infer, Pharaoh turns his madness inward. His command is
not only to all of Egypt to kill the Israelite boys whom the midwives
refused to destroy. Maddened by their refusal, he now turns reprisal
against his own people, commanding them to kill all boys, even
Egyptian ones!

Whether this is the intention of the text, it is certainly a possible
reading and fits the profile of such a maniac. Yet the later rabbis note
a moment of God's grace even in this extreme. They point out that
had Pharaoh ordered the girls to be killed, it would have been the
end of the Israelites and so the end of Jewish history, for without
women there could be no subsequent births.

Taking another tack, a fifth-century commentary on Genesis
links Pharaoh's choice of killing the males but saving the females to
Abraham's astonishing interlude in Egypt with his wife, Sarah. In
Genesis 12, Abraham worries that if the Egyptians believe Sarah to
be his wife, they will kill him and take her for themselves. The fifth-
century commentary offers this passage as proof that Abraham's
otherwise dubious scheme was, in fact, well founded. They did kill
the men and keep alive the women. A twelfth-century commentary
on our passage of Exodus makes clear the scurrilous nature of this
suggestion: "It was Pharaoh's intention to take the women into his
harem, for the Egyptians were steeped in immorality." As far as the
rabbis are concerned, killing boys wasn't enough. Pharaoh and his

Egyptians were so evil that they also prostituted the women they kept alive.

But enough Egypt bashing for the moment, there will still be plenty of that to come as the Exodus story unfolds. I wish to focus for a bit on the midwives, for determining the identities of Mss. Shifra and Pu'ah will help us determine some of the broader outlines of both the Exodus narrative and its readership. The Exodus text has Pharaoh commanding "the midwives of the Hebrews." Although we do know their names, the Hebrew is as unclear as the English translation as to the nationality of these midwives. It could be that they were Egyptian midwives who delivered Hebrew women. Or it could equally well be Hebrew midwives delivering Hebrew women. Now, this small detail may not seem important at first blush, but it caught the attention of rabbinic commentators already fifteen hundred years ago, and their debate was echoed in one of my own study groups just this year.

We sit in the Time-Life building, as we have for five years now, once a month in the boardroom of a powerful real estate company. Over dinner we study Bible. For three years (and two before that in a Madison Avenue office) we read our way through Genesis. Now we have moved on, ever so slowly, to Exodus. We spent almost an entire hour debating the identity of these midwives. Here's the crux of the matter: If the midwives were Jews, why did Pharaoh talk to them at all? Why not delegate a lesser officer to speak to slaves. The other side of the argument asks, If they were Egyptians, why did they disobey Pharaoh at all?

To the side that assumes a Jewish identity for the midwives, there is some further evidence. The midwives fear God. God rewards them. They keep the Jewish people alive. More narrowly, the Jewish women trust them as midwives. There is no xenophobia at this precious moment of vulnerability. Jews care for other Jews. Of course they oppose Pharaoh's crazy plan to murder. And as for Pharaoh commanding them in the first place, we remember only too sadly that sometimes people collaborate against their own for the favor of a tyrant. It happened in the concentration camps. And there, as perhaps here, a great deal was to be gained by the evil tyrant. His hands stay "clean." He is not directly engaged in the messy executions. Further, he has involved the very race he wishes to destroy without involving any of his own people. As it were, even as he destroys the babies, he rends the moral fabric of the people by implicating them in his crime.

But back to the other side of the argument. Is it not easier to enlist your own in the murder of the enemy? Pharaoh was no fool, surely he understood that Jewish women might not be inclined to obey him at all, let alone to obey a command to murder their own. So Pharaoh turns to the Egyptians, his subjects, and enlists their aid in eliminating the Jewish vermin. He obviously does not bank on his Egyptians fearing God. After all, is not Pharaoh himself a god to the Egyptians? Is the Exodus text then trying to show us that there are righteous gentiles? Women who will assert their solidarity with other women over any command? Women who will honor their vows to bring life, not death? Women who recognize the moral imperative of the God of Israel and reject the murderous schemes of Pharaoh?

But if the midwives were Jews, we may argue, it is a tighter story. After all, the Bible is a Jewish book, isn't it? It is about how Jews protect Jews, and that is the lesson it is teaching. Some rabbis of ancient times go as far as to equate Shifra and Pu'ah, otherwise unknown, with the two central women who will emerge in Moses' family, his mother, Yocheved, and his sister, Miriam. This reading makes Exodus even more insular. It is about the Moses family and their heroics. The "households" God provides as reward for their refusal of Pharaoh is leadership of Israel. Good reward for a day's midwifery. But a very narrow reading of the tale.

But then again, if the midwives are Egyptians after all, we have to wonder who this story is meant to appeal to and what are the lessons it teaches. Are non-Jews supposed to read about the gentile midwives and cheer them on, applaud their resolve to oppose evil, learn a moral lesson from them? Shall Egyptians read of the Egyptian midwives and react like the Germans did to the viewing of *Schindler's List,* delighted to find a Good German as moral exemplar, even if fifty years after the fact? Is Exodus really for non-Jews to read and identify with? Shall we suggest that the lessons of this book are universal, meant to appeal to the downtrodden everywhere? Could the story of redemption be a story for everybody?

More broadly, whose Bible is it anyway? Do you have to be Jewish to appreciate and identify with Exodus? Could this book be *meant* for readers beyond the Jewish community? It is read by Christians, certainly, but Jews sometimes feel queasy about it, as though the Torah has been usurped. African Americans read of slavery and freedom and see Exodus as their own story. In past decades, Jews were comfortable sharing this legacy with the black community. Even broader, what of readers who are not Jewish or Christian? Can Muslims read this story and, once they are past the difficulty that it is Egypt (a Muslim country) playing the role of heavy in this drama, can they, too, claim this universal narrative as their own? If so, how about Buddhists, Zoroastrians, Hindus, atheists? Might the very message of the Exodus narrative hint that the book is both universal as well as particularist? I believe it well might.

Those midwives deliver a great deal more than babies when the discussion takes this kind of turn. But the debate is appropriate to the story. It *is* a very particular story of how one family, the children of Israel, came into covenant with God following their redemption from slavery. It is a story, *the story,* of chosenness. And it is the story of how all people still benefit from the tale. How everyone has something to gain from opposition to tyranny and overthrow of godless injustice.

In the end, it makes little difference whether the midwives were Jewish, Egyptian, or anything else. What matters is that they saved the lives they were meant to destroy. They were rewarded for their fear of God, or what we would identify as moral courage. We give thanks for their delivery, in every sense of the word, to this very day.

THE
NAKED
WOMAN ON
WALL STREET

I n a border town on the far eastern edge of the Roman
Empire, some 1,740 years ago, Persian soldiers held the
garrison of Dura-Europos under siege. The town was
nestled on the western banks of the Euphrates River in
what is today eastern Syria. To the north and south the
town was protected by deep wadis, ravines that fell
away steeply from Dura's walls. Only the western aspect of the
city lay exposed, and there the Persian troops patiently
encamped. Within the town, pains were taken to keep firmly
closed the great gate of that long western wall, a gate double
the height of a man on camelback. The buildings on the town's
western edge ran close to the wall, a narrow street separated

them from the only thing keeping the Persians out. Naturally, when Yale University archaeologists excavated Dura some seventeen centuries later, they would name this path "Wall Street."

As the Romans inside Dura grew ever more alarmed at their fate, they filled in Wall Street with rubble, the better to strengthen the wall that was keeping the Persians at bay. Once that project was completed, one by one they poured sand and rubble into the western portions of each building facing Wall Street, to further buttress what little protection the wall offered against the troops massed outside. In the end, all defenses failed, the Sassanian Persians overran Dura-Europos, sacked the city, and, soon after, abandoned it. Already partially filled in with sand and rubble at the hands of the Roman defenders, wind, sand, and storm completed the work of burying the city from sight. Then, in 1920, British troops discovered wall paintings and roused the interests of archaeologists and art historians. From 1922 through 1937, particularly during the last decade of that period, archaeologists from Yale University carefully dug up Dura-Europos, a treasure trove that displayed the crossroads of two empires, Roman and Persian, at their zeniths.

Thanks to the protective layers of sand and soil first shoveled in by the Romans in 256 C.E., the buildings of Wall Street, particularly the western walls of those buildings, were well preserved for the scrutiny of twentieth-century eyes. The buildings included five pagan temples, a Christian chapel, and a Roman bath. Imagine how wide the excavators' eyes opened when a few blocks north of the great gate a synagogue was uncovered, the walls of which were covered floor to ceiling with frescoes. Rich color drawings of biblical characters and scenes were unearthed with every passing day. From November 1932 through October 1934, almost every day of digging and the careful brushing away of debris revealed new frescoes, many with Greek captions, as the synagogue came into view. Even as the synagogues of Europe entered a decade of murderous darkness, the synagogue of Dura-Europos on the banks of the Euphrates came into brilliant light.

Perhaps the most startling of the Dura-Europos paintings is found among the reredos of the western wall of the synagogue. There, oriented as it is toward the Holy Land and Jerusalem, is a neatly centered shell-shaped shrine, which no doubt housed a Torah scroll. The reredos, paintings that adorn the wall behind the shrine, richly illustrate the history of biblical Israel. To the right, above the Torah shrine, is a fresco of Moses at the burning bush. Just below that, a male holds a scroll open in his hands. Most likely the scroll is a Torah. It is also likely that this fellow, cloaked in Greek garb, is again meant to be Moses. Below him, two pictures to the right of the shrine and running all the way to the north wall is yet another picture of Moses.

This last fresco is the object of my fascination here. It is the oldest picture of Moses in existence. The background paint was deep red when first uncovered, it has since faded to brownish earth tones. There are three separate scenes in the frescoed panel. In each of them is Moses as the baby in the basket. In the center panel, attended by three servants at her toilet, the woman who fished Moses out of the river and set him on his life's journey stands stark naked in the water of the Nile. In the earliest sketches we have from the Dura excavations she is naked, and the baby in her arms has had no features painted onto his face (in later reproductions he has a face and she a bikini!). In a picture to the left, the baby is held jointly by two robed women, an older and a younger, their hair piously covered by veils. To the right, the woman from the water, now dressed, is accompanied by those two women as she bows low, presenting the baby to a man seated on a throne, attended by two courtiers.

Certainly every Shabbat and possibly daily, the Jews of Dura-Europos gazed at the naked woman on Wall Street and contemplated the fate of Moses. In doing so, they perhaps contemplated their own fates—also at a mighty river's shore, their religious distinctiveness clear yet nevertheless equally submerged as but one part of a great foreign empire. A millennium and a half ago and more, on the border between Rome and Persia, the Jews of Dura-Europos had plenty of time to think about their own identities and that of their law-giver Moses, who a millennium and a half before them found himself submerged—first in the River Nile and then in the very court of Pharaoh.

> When she could no longer hide him, she took a reed basket for him and daubed it with pitch and bitumen. She placed the boy in the basket and put it in the reeds at the bank of the River Nile. His sister

stood watch from afar that she might know what would be done to him. The daughter of Pharaoh had descended to bathe in the Nile, her servants attending on the bank. She saw the basket in the midst of the reeds and sent her maid to fetch it. When she opened it she saw the baby, it was a boy, crying! She took pity on him and said, "This one is a child of the Hebrews."

Then his sister said to the daughter of Pharaoh, "Shall I go and call a wet-nurse woman from the Hebrews that she may suckle the child for you?"

The daughter of Pharaoh said to her, "Go!" So the young woman went and called the boy's mother. The daughter of Pharaoh said to her, "Go, take this child and suckle him for me, I will give you your reward."

So the woman took the boy and nursed him. When the boy grew up she brought him to the daughter of Pharaoh. He was a son to her and she called his name Moses [*Moshe*], saying, from the water I have drawn him [*mesheiteihu*]. (Exod. 2:3–10)

The panels of the Dura-Europos synagogue should be clear now. In the center, the naked lady is Pharaoh's daughter, who, attended by her maidservants, is fetching the child Moses from the River Nile. To the left, jointly holding baby Moses are his sister, Miriam, who had been keeping an eye on him all the while he was afloat, and Moses' mother, Yocheved, who would wet-nurse him and raise him until he was weaned. The final picture in the panel shows us Pharaoh's daughter along with Miriam and Yocheved, the three women of Moses' youth. They present him to Pharaoh, who is flanked by courtiers. This, need I remind you, is the same Pharaoh who had commanded the drowning of Jewish baby boys. Now, in the presence of his court and the presence of two nice Jewish girls, he finds himself a grandfather by adoption to a cute little Jewish boy. An interesting moment, this, and right there on a synagogue wall for everyone to mull over. Daily, the Jews of Dura must have mused, God certainly works in strange ways.

Strange indeed, and wonderful, modern readers also muse. For there can be no question that Pharaoh's daughter is complicit in a plot to disobey her father, much as were the midwives. She says out loud, before her servants, "This one is a child of the Hebrews."

When Moses' sister, Miriam, hovering nearby, offers a wet-nurse, she, too, tips her hand with "a Hebrew woman." A rabbinic commentary just a century or so after the time of the Dura synagogue suggests that baby Moses had by then already made the rounds of the Egyptian wet-nurses and refused to suckle at any of their breasts. So, as the only expedient, Pharaoh's daughter had to rely on a Hebrew wet-nurse. Rabbi Hama bar Hanina, a contemporary of the Duran frescoes, suggested that Yocheved's righteousness is what merited the return of her son. Not only that, he adds, but she was rewarded, too!

What are we to make of this conspiracy? Is this women's solidarity? The midwives seem to lead the way and other women follow. They will not succumb to Pharaoh's mad demands. The women will be life givers, not life takers. They will hide Jewish babies, raise them as their own. It is reminiscent of the Righteous Gentiles who defied Nazi Germany and saved Jewish children. Yet here, Pharaoh's daughter not only flouts his decree, she flaunts it in his very palace. "Here, Daddy," we imagine her saying, "a new grandson for your pleasure." Does the old man not notice that the baby is circumcised?

Of course, it is possible that Moses is not circumcised, but the rabbis think otherwise. How would Pharaoh's daughter have known with such assurance that Moses was a child of the Hebrews when she looked into the basket on the river? For that matter, how could any rabbi imagine that Moses, of all people, could *not* have been circumcised? Some modern scholars have suggested that Egyptians, too, circumcised their children. So perhaps we need not peek too carefully at baby Moses swaddled in his basket. It surely was enough for Pharaoh's daughter simply to infer that a baby adrift on the Nile must have been abandoned in the face of her father's decree. She did not have to be a rocket scientist to make the deduction that such a child is a Hebrew.

But this does not obviate the presence of the boy in Pharaoh's home. Circumcised or not, there is this baby in the palace. It is difficult to know whether Pharaoh's daughter was married or single. If she were married, we might remotely imagine that the old man was sufficiently distant from the affairs of the harem to be unaware that one of his daughters (she was only a girl, after all) was pregnant. Yet in our imagination, it is all too easy to see her as a single woman, perhaps even an only child, bringing Pharaoh a potential heir to his throne. Were that the case, he surely would have cause to wonder and to investigate. "My daughter has a baby? By whom? Adopted? From whom? Oh, a *Jewish* baby! Delightful. Bring the little tyke here so I can hug him."

Indeed, a twelfth-century midrash imagines just that. Evil as Pharaoh may be in Jewish memory, at that moment he was a new grandfather. The midrash explains: "Pharaoh's daughter would kiss and hug and love that baby as though he were her own. She wouldn't let him out of that palace. Since he was so cute, everyone longed to see him. And once they laid eyes on him, they didn't want to let him go. So Pharaoh came to kiss him and hug him, so much that the baby would reach up and take off Pharaoh's crown to play with and put it on his own head."

The symbolism of this story, heavy-handed though it may be, should not pass unnoticed. God brings the one who will overthrow Pharaoh onto his very lap and has him remove the crown from his head. Pharaoh, guilty of killing infants, will be brought down by the baby he himself loved. The irony of this rabbinic legend is all the more replete in a more baroque version of its telling. In this second version, Pharaoh's courtiers see the ill omen that is portended with the baby's removal of Pharaoh's crown. They urge him to be careful, not to trust this child. They wish to put baby Moses to a test of his innocence. And so, in this rabbinic telling of the tale, they place baby Moses in a playpen with Grandpa's shiny crown in one corner and a glowing coal in another. If the baby is only attracted by the glitter, he can reach for the coal. If, however, he means to harm Pharaoh, he will again reach for the crown, and then they will dispose of him. And so the baby goes crawling toward the shiny objects in the playpen. At the last moment the angel Gabriel pushes baby Moses' pudgy hand to the coal, thus saving his life and the future of the people Israel. Yet the price is a burned hand, which the infant, in a universal reaction, sticks into his mouth to soothe. The coal, still clutched, burns Moses' tongue. When the baby grows up and talks he will have a speech impediment. Indeed, this very disability is reported by Moses in Exodus 4:10, when he complains to God, "I am slow of speech and slow tongued."

We will return to Moses growing up in Pharaoh's court shortly. For now we should focus on the two other scenes depicted on the wall mural and in our passage of Exodus. First, we return to the baby in the basket. Set adrift by his desperate parents he is providentially guided to float into the hands of Pharaoh's daughter. We may well recall Joseph's comments in Genesis about his own good fortune in Egypt, "It was God who sent me here and put me as a father to Pharaoh, as master of his house and ruler of all the Land of Egypt" (Gen. 45:8). Moses could just as well recite that quote about himself, stopping only to change the word *father* to the word *grandson*.

What are we to make of Pharaoh's daughter, a nameless girl/woman, a princess of Egypt. She saves the baby and becomes Moses' adoptive mother. We must remember the story in Genesis of Sarah (Hebrew for "princess") and her Egyptian maid Hagar. The latter was to have been a birth mother so that Sarah might take her child and raise him as her own. Now, a Jewish mother gives up her baby to an Egyptian princess. Is this but a case of literary reversal as the plot so carefully stitched in Genesis comes unraveled in Exodus?

Then there is Miriam, our prophetic big sister. She hangs in there and engineers her brother's (and the people Israel's) salvation. Not only does she see him safely into Pharaoh's daughter's hand, but she bravely steps forward to reveal herself to offer a wet-nurse from the Hebrews. When she runs and brings the baby's (and her own) mother, does not Pharaoh's daughter sense the plot? Is Pharaoh's daughter so consumed by baby hunger that she knowingly strikes a bargain with the birth mother—you suckle him, I'll raise him and keep him alive?

Can Yocheved have been strong enough and brave enough to have agreed to the deal? We know she was willing to take the risk of hiding the baby. We know she was willing to take the risk of setting him afloat on the Nile. We can be sure she eagerly suckled him. But could she have had a stout enough heart after weaning him to give him away? Was this the only way to guarantee his survival? A late Yemenite midrash has Yocheved fearful even to suckle the child. After all, Pharaoh has decreed death to Jewish baby boys. What if they find her with her own son? Will they not all be at risk? Thus does Pharaoh's daughter reassure her in the words of Exodus, "take this child and suckle him for me." The midrash emphasizes those last two words: "for me." It is as though Pharaoh's daughter tells her, "since it will clearly be for me, you will be protected from harm."

And so, Yocheved brings Moses home after his adventure on the Nile. Home to his father, Amram; his brother, Aaron; and his protective sister, Miriam. Home to be suckled at his mother's breast, to imbibe the warmth of family and Jewish values along with mother's milk. How long does the idyll continue? How long can Yocheved continue the charade of keeping the growing boy in her home when all the other Jewish boys have vanished? How long can Pharaoh's daughter hold out before she reclaims as her own the child she has saved?

What does Pharaoh's daughter really know of the arrangement she has made with Miriam and Yocheved? Does she realize they are the baby's immediate family? Surely she may suspect this. If so, will she give them visitation rights once she has taken the child into Pharaoh's court? Or is it too much to imagine the Jews trooping in to visit Moses as he grows to become an Egyptian courtier?

How much does Moses himself know? How old is he when he is finally given over to Pharaoh's daughter and Pharaoh's court? The rabbis, probably extrapolating from their own customs, assume him to be two years old when he is transferred from home to court. Just about the age most American children begin full-time day care. Is Moses toilet trained? Does he speak Hebrew already? Just how aware is a two-year-old of his upbringing? But does the narrator of Exodus assume Moses has an awareness of his Hebrew identity? Does Pharaoh's daughter tell him he is an adopted child of the Hebrews?

What is it like to grow up Moses in Pharaoh's court? A lot depends, I suppose, on what Moses knows of his origins and, perhaps, when he learns it. If he grows up thinking all along that he is a natural son of Pharaoh's daughter, he will grow up with a sense of privilege and power that may not be pretty. He might be spoiled, arrogant, all the things one would expect of a young prince in the court of Pharaoh. Of course, there will be those in the court who will know his secret. They may disdain him—providing there is no great risk of Pharaoh's wrath. Much depends upon how Moses is treated by his adoptive grandfather.

A fifth-century commentary suggests that Moses' assimilation was complete. After all, the Exodus text explicitly says of his relationship with the daughter of Pharaoh, "he was a son to her." Hence, the midrash suggests that "he was elevated to the rank of Comes Calator." A nice touch, since the fifth-century rabbis anachronize and give Moses the Latin title of the member of the Roman Emperor's court who is the Count of State Banquets, a kind of chief of protocol and chief of staff all rolled into one. The point of the midrash is that Moses had access, he came and went in Pharaoh's court, he was a member of the inner circle.

Of course, there is always that nagging feeling that this is only one side of the coin. We are told repeatedly in Scripture of Moses' humility: "The man Moses was very humble." Perhaps this modesty and possibly even low sense of self-worth found its origins in Pharaoh's household. Maybe Moses knew he was adopted and, like many adoptees, felt insecure about his origins. Perhaps he wondered why his birth parents abandoned him, no matter how much wealth and power he had been delivered to. It could be he looked physically different than the noble Egyptians. Maybe he was darker, maybe lighter. Maybe his Semitic nose was more hooked, less aquiline. Maybe he looked exactly like every other courtier, but his speech impediment set him apart. Or maybe the speech impediment was a stutter, a psychological artifact of his own feelings of inadequacy and difference.

Moses the man is also representative of the Jewish people here. The Torah is quintessentially a book about diaspora Jewry. It is a book about longing for the Promised Land, a land only briefly experienced yet yearned for, particularly from Egypt. And Egypt is a diaspora where for a long time the Jews flourished. First, they flourished under Joseph. Then, even Moses flourished. But underneath the successes of those leaders is the horrible reality of Jewish enslavement. It is difficult to read the Torah now without reflecting on Jewish experience in Europe. Enlightenment brought many benefits to the Jews. They were citizens, apparently equal partners; they flourished. Yet no Jew could forget the Inquisition, or the Expulsions, or, more recently, the Holocaust. However successful Moses may be in Pharaoh's court, to the extent that he still has even a shred of Jewish identity, he must be nervous. All his power cannot obviate the fact of his people's slavery, just outside the door.

Moses is everyman. For not only Jews have had to contend with success, enlightenment, assimilation—all the while being marked as different. This is also the history of African Americans, Armenians, Serbian Muslims, virtually every minority in every country in every era. Is it any wonder that for millennia people everywhere have looked to Moses and the Exodus as a paradigmatic myth of redemption?

The essence of this story comes at the moment Moses recognizes that he may be a grandee in Pharaoh's palace, but his people are elsewhere—outside, enslaved. Whether it is an adolescent search for birth parents, or a recognition that he is an outsider masquerading as an insider, or a spiritual longing, a need for belonging—at some moment everything changes. The pampered garb of his youth is thrown off and the mantle of leadership, a greatness hedged by his innate humility, is accepted. At that moment Moses can no longer stay within the walls of the palace—they feel too much like besieged Dura, doomed to oblivion—he must go out and seek his future.

THE
FUGITIVE

So it happened in those days that Moses grew and went out to his brothers to see their burdens. He saw an Egyptian man striking a Hebrew man of his brethren. He turned this way and that and saw there was no man. So he struck the Egyptian and hid him in the sand.

He went out the next day and two Hebrew men were fighting. He said to the offender, "Why do you strike your fellow?"

He replied, "Who made you the man, a prince who judges us? Do you express to kill me like you killed the Egyptian?"

Moses was fearful and said, "Oh, the matter is known!"

Then Pharaoh heard of the matter and wished to kill Moses. So
Moses fled from Pharaoh and dwelled in Midian, settling by the
well. (Exod. 2:11–15)

How long did Moses live in Pharaoh's court before he "went out
to his brothers" and set the wheel of his fate aspin? There are so
many unanswered questions raised here in these five verses. Again,
Exodus is short on narrative, long on omission. We do not know
whether Moses knew of his Judaism all along or some particular
event sparked his interest. We do not know if he grew to feel guilty
of his luxurious existence while his brethren suffered. We do not
even know if Moses was aware that his brothers, the Israelites, were
the slaves building Pharaoh's empire, although it must have been
hard not to know that fact.

The ancient rabbis loved symmetry, so when they read this narrative, frustrated as we are at the lack of detail, they filled in the blanks
with some elegance. A second-century midrash seizes on the biblical
report that Moses was eighty when he stood before Pharaoh to
demand Israel's release from slavery. We know that Moses was 120
at his death. Therefore, the rule of symmetry demands that if he
spent forty years leading the Israelites, he would also be forty when
he goes out to see his brothers and sets the plot in motion. Forty
years in Pharaoh's court, forty as a shepherd in Midian, forty leading
the Jews through the Sinai wilderness.

A certain rabbi, also named Moses, who lived in Narbonne in the
eleventh century, took his symmetry a different way and suggested
that our Moses was at midlife, sixty, when he "went out to his brothers." An anonymous twelfth-century rabbi, perhaps worried lest
Moses seem too content in Pharaoh's household and possibly seem
unconcerned about his birth family, suggests that Moses was but
twenty when he went on his fateful visit. This latter suggestion might
account for the immature violence of his reaction to the Egyptian
taskmaster. I suppose, however, that the guilt of sitting pretty for
forty or sixty years might also account for Moses' homicidal reaction.

Of course, in rabbinic tradition Moses is hardly criticized at all.
The rabbis, instead, show their concern for his murder of the Egyp-
tian by jumping to his defense. They take Scripture's description of
Moses' turning "this way and that" not as a sign that he was worried

that what he would do might be observed and considered wrong. Rather, he turns this way and that in his consideration of the Egyptian's guilt, and he determines to the satisfaction of human and divine law that surely this Egyptian merits the death penalty. For the moment, let us rest content with this traditional defense of Moses' actions. We will return to his striking the Egyptian below, for it seems an important test of Moses' character and leadership ability. Is this the act of a just and rational authority, or is it the irrational acting out of an insecure man pursued by demons of guilt? This seems to be a question that merits careful consideration, particularly in a society (ours) that agonizes so profoundly and publicly over the moral character of our leaders.

Great leaders inspire confidence and emulation. Whether it is a Mahatma Gandhi, Martin Luther King, or FDR in this century (or any other pantheon of heroes you choose), we look to them as examples. We desire to know the details of their lives so that we might learn the secret of their success. What seminal events shaped them? Whether it was their childhood, their schooling, a lost election—all of these details fascinate, for they may hold the key to the character of great leadership. Yet the book of Exodus shows us so little of Moses. We only know that he spent time growing up in Pharaoh's court; we do not even know how long a time it took for him to "come out" as an Israelite. And, as we will read later in this chapter, he lives in exile for a time after he kills the Egyptian taskmaster. Again, we do not know for how long. All we see, the only details the Bible reveals, are those few before us.

We must assume, then, that the storyteller of Exodus judges these details relevant to Moses' growth as the future leader of Israel. His act of retribution and its consequences somehow shape the development of the Moses we will eventually see stand before Pharaoh to demand freedom for the Israelites. But not yet. The Moses we see before us now has just killed an Egyptian and buried him in the sand. And the Israelites reject Moses, burying their heads ostrich-like, as it were, in the sand. They cannot see the details of Moses' development as their champion any better than we can. Nevertheless, they judge him.

Before we judge Moses' retributive act against the Egyptian, we should try to see what he witnessed there in Egypt. What were "the burdens" of the Jews and what was the nature of their slavery? What was Moses' perception of what he observed? Could it have affected his murderous reaction? We have already learned that what Moses saw was slavery, hard labor at building and in the fields. Ancient commentators, perhaps with an eye to Moses' reaction, suggest that the Egyptian overseers sexually abused Israelite women while their men were performing these very labors. We know from our own country's history that it is not unusual for a master to so treat his female slaves. It is not unreasonable to assume such degradation took place in pharaonic Egypt. Conveniently, adulterous rape is a capital crime in later Israelite law, so the assignment of this crime to the Egyptian taskmaster also serves to exculpate Moses' reaction.

Other commentators, with an eye to Moses' future leadership, suggest that when Moses saw their labors he reacted to his Israelite brethren with sympathy. Some rabbis have Moses carrying their burdens alongside the Hebrew slaves. Others even have him crying at the sight of their oppression. I confess that each of these readings sounds suspiciously like modern liberal reactions to the sorrows of the underclasses. While I heartily endorse these as possibilities, one must wonder how the Israelite slaves perceived Moses' initial reaction to them. It is easy to imagine they viewed his sudden liberal interest with a somewhat jaundiced eye.

Psychologist Dr. Ian Miller suggested to me that the reaction of the Israelites is not incidental here. This is not just the story of Moses, far from it; it is the story of how a people rose from slavery to have a covenant with God. The reaction of the anonymous Israelites is, as such, most instructive. It is easy, Dr. Miller suggested, to react against slavery. But to react negatively to one of your own who suddenly asserts leadership—a leadership that may be good intentioned but might, in fact, be dangerous for the slaves—has the effect of unifying the Israelites. Although initially opposed to Moses, their very opposition disposes them to become a people.

My response to Ian Miller was to theologize this reaction. The Israelites learn to oppose human leadership because, in the end, they have no leader but God, the Creator with whom they come into covenant. Dr. Miller was not quite so sanguine. Opposition to leadership is a caricature of the Jews. When faced with upper-crust leadership they react almost comically, "Who made you the man, a prince who judges us?" Miller has been a member of the Jewish community all his life, he knows only too well how we treat our erstwhile leadership. Yet his observation of group process, an area of psychology that is his specialty, is trenchant.

Who was this pretender who came down from the palace to make trouble? The death of an Egyptian overseer, while a momentary victory, could only spell disaster over time. Further, did these enslaved Jews recognize Moses as one of their own? If so, they must wonder what took him so damn long to emerge from the palace. And once the act is done, he returns to the palace! Enough of that nonsense. Slaves have little patience for liberal foolishness. Moses' rebuke the next day of one of his own brethren must have been the last straw for them. We should have some sympathy for the enslaved Israelites; nobody likes "the man." It was too easy for the oppressed to read Moses as an "Oreo," an Uncle Tom. Their opposition to his sudden assertion of leadership, his insertion into "their" affairs could only have been anathema. It will take Moses a long time to earn his stripes as the leader of the Jews.

To the extent that we might understand the slaves as having a "gang" mentality, his murder of the Egyptian was an essential first step on the road to leadership. Transforming the gang of slaves into a covenant people would be a journey of equal length and labor. In the meantime, the beginning of that transformation comes when the slaves act as a group. The anonymous voice of the two fighting Israelites articulates their unity in opposition to outside leadership being imposed upon them. First they must become fugitives from leadership. Only then, when they cohere in that opposition, can they escape Egypt and become fugitive slaves. This dual role as fugitives eventually will lead them to Sinai, where they can take shelter under God's protective suzerainty.

Moses can foresee none of this. He reacts in the moment, first to the Egyptian brutalizing his newly found brothers. Next, he reacts to his brothers brutalizing one another. Here, too, while naive, Moses' leadership instincts are apparent. He knows that his brethren will remain slaves so long as they fight among themselves. He knows that this internal strife is what keeps them at one another's throats rather than focusing them to unite against the brutality of the Egyptians. He may even know that it is the very oppression of the Egyptians that serves to divide the Israelites and pit them against one another. What he cannot foresee is that his intervention will cause them to turn against him.

As I suggested above, my friend Ian Miller is on the right track. The turn against Moses is the start of a turn against Egypt. If they can oppose "the man" from the palace whom they also know to be their brother, eventually they can oppose Pharaoh. As it turns out, perhaps providentially, Moses' dual acts of leadership and judgment—his killing of the Egyptian and his intervening in the Israelite dispute—are the acts that set the eventual freedom of the Israelites into motion. A fair time must pass until the freedom is brought to fruition, but the beginning of that process is the moment the slave says to Moses, "Who made you the man?"

What Moses does see, however, is just how far Israel is from freedom. A twelfth-century commentary perceptively imagines Moses recognizing the disability the slave people suffer. When he is queried by the quarreling slaves whether he intends to do to them as he did to the Egyptian, the Bible has Moses exclaim, "Oh! The matter is known!" *Midrash Exodus Rabbah* expands this interior monologue by having Moses realize that the word has spread among the slave camp. With a strong faith in Moses' piety the midrash quotes a certain Rabbi Yehudah, who tells us: Moses was fretting trying to understand why the Israelites had been enslaved in the first place. When he realized that they committed the sin of gossip, he despaired that they would ever be freed.

This is a perspicacious reading. While it recognizes Moses' fear at being discovered, it also reveals great understanding of the slave mentality. The only currency they have to pass around is gossip. As we all know, the more vicious, the more valuable the gossip. If this is the coin of the Israelite realm, there is virtually no hope for them. Gossip is a symptom of an unhealthy social structure. When members of the group take their pleasure in tearing one another down, there can be no moral structure to support them. Without mutual support there can be no effective opposition to external forces. Is it any wonder that at that moment Moses despairs?

The rest of the scene is but denouement. His embrace rejected by his newly acknowledged brothers, Moses cannot go back. Having killed an Egyptian, Moses breaks with his palace past and the protection it offered him. Not a slave, but no longer an Egyptian, Moses has no place to hide. That the Torah has Pharaoh turn against him is no surprise. Yet we must wonder if merely plot drives this wrenching turn against Moses.

If Moses had been an Egyptian, if he had been Pharaoh's birth grandson rather than an adoptive one, would Pharaoh have sought to kill Moses? The word of a courtier should surely suffice against any report of the death of an Egyptian slave driver. It cannot have been so unusual for the men of Pharaoh's households to have had violent reprisals against their underlings—at least if pharaonic Egypt was as cruel as later biblical perception paints it. The men of the palace protect their own in any case. So why Pharaoh's sudden desire to kill Moses?

This is not unrelated to Moses' own return to his slave-brothers on the morrow. For Moses the murder was an irrevocable break with his adopted past. His choice of sympathy with the Israelites was not a momentary one, but a life-changing decision. There really was no going back to the palace for Moses. If so, Pharaoh could only view Moses as a traitor. He has not only killed a representative of the Egyptian regime, he has rejected his past. The years of nurture given to him by his adoptive family were overthrown. The protections class and palace offered were rudely shoved aside. An entire civilization has been spurned by this Moses. Pharaoh's wrath must be unleashed. One cannot reject a god without consequence!

Moses, raised in the court, perceives all this and more in the instant he buries the Egyptian in the sand. Moses is, in fact, burying Egyptian civilization and all it represents at that moment. He is "the man." And he acts as a "a prince who judges." But it is not merely the cruel taskmaster Moses judges, it is Egypt, particularly Egypt as it is incarnate in Pharaoh. Moses cannot go home to the palace for he has chosen his home with the very slaves the palace oppresses. Nor, however, can he go home to those slaves. They themselves reject him. Further, to be among them as an enemy of Pharaoh is to make their lot even worse. It is bad enough for the Israelites, Moses cannot expect them to also harbor Pharaoh's enemy. At least not yet.

The Israelites are fugitives from leadership; they are, after all, slaves. Moses, then, must be a fugitive from Pharaoh and, for the time being, a fugitive from his own people. He flees to Midian and takes refuge by "the well." The same twelfth-century midrash that commented on Israel's penchant for gossip has a keen take on the well. The rabbis of the midrash, careful readers of Scripture that they were, have read enough of Genesis to know that when a biblical character travels to a well, take note. In particular, wells serve as the scene for romance. So, despite Moses' fugitive character at this moment, his settling by the well alerts us. As the midrash has it, locating Moses firmly in the traditions of his ancestors, "Three drew their mates from 'the well.' Isaac (see Genesis 24:62–67), Jacob (see Genesis 29:2–20), and Moses."

So even as Moses flees Egypt, we may rest assured that at least *he* will come into the bosom of family. Even as Moses leaves behind Pharaoh's court and his adoptive mother, he will find at the well a new home to nurture him. Even as Moses leaves his brothers enslaved, he turns to a new chapter of his life.

It, too, has its ambiguities, not the least of which must be Moses' twofold worry. First, he is a fugitive from Pharaoh. Second, he has abandoned his people in a way more complete than when he lived in Pharaoh's palace. At least there he could pretend that one day he might go out and claim them as his own. There he might imagine he could succeed Pharaoh and free the slaves. Now he can no longer fantasize. He has been rejected by Pharaoh and by his own people. There is no turning back. There is only the well. Moses, once courtier to Pharaoh, has only the well in Midian to sustain him as he hides. And while we, the readers, may know that the well portends romance and family, Moses can, at this low moment of his life, only despair. A fugitive from the palace and Pharaoh, a fugitive from his people who have rejected him, lost from his family whether by birth, adoption, or marriage, Moses is at his nadir when he flees to the well.

> As it happened, the priest of Midian had seven daughters. Now they came to the well and drew water, filling the troughs in order to water their father's sheep. When the shepherds came and drove them out, Moses arose and saved them and watered their flocks. When they came back to their father Reuel he asked them, "How did you return so quickly today?"

They answered, "An Egyptian man rescued us from the shepherds and then drew water for us and watered the sheep."

He asked his daughters, "So where is he? Why did you leave that man? Invite him to break bread with us!"

Moses promised to dwell with the man, who gave his daughter Tzipporah to Moses. She bore a son whom he called Gershom [stranger there] for he said, "I be a stranger in a foreign land." (Exod. 2:16–22)

Thus Moses begins his second exile. His first, in Pharaoh's palace, was dislocating. He grew under the tutelage of the palace courtiers, thinking himself one of them yet knowing he was different. Ultimately, as we saw above, he returned to his people and left the palace behind. Yet in short order he was forced to flee Egypt entirely to seek safety in the land of Midian. In a classic well scene, much like Jacob's in Genesis 29, Moses once again reveals himself a champion of the underdog. This time there is no homicide, merely the humble business of watering the sheep. In short order Moses settles in, marries, has a son.

Yet even as we breathe a sigh of relief that all is well at the well, the biblical text carries disconcerting clues to undermine our complacency. Yes, Moses, who by rights can think of himself as a prince of Egypt—as a Yemenite midrash explains—humbles himself by not only rescuing strange girls but then by the demeaning labor of watering their flocks. Yet beyond that humility things are not quite right. The helpless girls, at the mercy of the shepherds, in fact have a father who is the local priest. One would expect that they would be afforded some respect. Instead, they require rescue.

And Moses himself is first abandoned by the girls. Only when their father insists do they bring him home. They identify him as an Egyptian—a nice irony, for how could they think him otherwise? As it turns out, not only is he not an Egyptian, but their hero is on Egypt's most-wanted list. Even worse, he's a Hebrew, kinsmen to the slaves of Egypt. Perhaps not such a hot match for the girls after all. By then it is too late. The anxious father, Reuel, later called Jethro, has married off his little bird Tzipporah (that's what her name means) and can only console himself with "funny, he didn't look Jewish."

So there is Moses, a stranger in a strange land, as the King James version so eloquently puts it. No longer in the Egypt where he grew up, nor in the land of Canaan promised to his ancestors, Moses languishes in Midian. The Torah seems unclear about this land of Midian. Even today there is a great deal of disagreement over exactly where Moses was when he fled Egypt and settled in Midian by the well. In Numbers 25, the Midianites seem to be anathema to the Jews, their women tempt the Israelite men away from God's proper worship. But in Genesis 25 they are listed as the offspring of Abraham, born to his late life trophy wife Keturah. To ice the cake of literary symbolism, it was the Midianites who brought Joseph down to slavery in Egypt and began this whole mess (Genesis 37:28).

It is important to remember Joseph at this juncture, for he, like Moses, spent a fair piece of his life in Pharaoh's palace. Like Moses, Joseph married "out" and gave his sons names indicative of his feelings of exile (see Genesis 41:51–52). We cannot help but hear the echoes of ancestral history that underscore Moses' feelings of alienation. Although settled in Midian, Moses takes up the life of a shepherd, wandering. Although raised in the palace, he now spends his days under the open sky. Although married with family, he is far from his own brothers and sisters. Although under the protection of his father-in-law, he battles other shepherds for the right to water his flocks. And Moses waits, a fugitive, for someone else to think him an Egyptian and report his whereabouts to the Pharaoh who seeks his life.

The ambiguities of his exile are most clear in the name he gives his son. Gershom means "stranger there," a name Moses explains to us, his readers. The trouble with the explanation is in the translation. For Hebrew does not have the same tenses as English. What I have rendered "I be a stranger" is an imperfect in Hebrew. What that means is that it is sometimes translated "I have been a stranger in a foreign land." The implication of that rendering might be that Moses was a stranger in Egypt, but now, in Midian with a family, he is a stranger no longer. But the other way it is translated is "I have become a stranger." That translation, of course, allows Moses to be nostalgic for pharaonic Egypt, for his adoptive home, for his physical proximity to his people. It means that his wife and son and the very flocks he shepherds are the things that make him feel foreign. "Imperfect" and "tense" are the words grammarians use to explain the verb that describes Moses in this verse. They capture his existential condition eloquently.

RUMINATING

Sheep crop close. That's why householders and most farmers do not care for them at all. Once sheep have grazed your land, nothing will grow back that year. A careless shepherd or a crafty one can run his flock over your land and let his sheep eat you out of house and home. So the shepherd was not warmly greeted and often not trusted. For his part, since the sheep did crop so close, he could not graze his flock in one place for very long. Shepherds had to be always on the move in search of fresh pasture. They spent a lot of time away from their own homes and family, always walking, always under the hot sun, never very welcome anywhere. And aside from the bleating company of sheep, they were almost always alone. Shepherds lived off the open land, but they lived inside their own heads, interior monologue their only company. They had lots of time to ruminate along with their sheep.

In part, the nomadic life of the shepherd accounts for our difficulty in pinpointing the location of biblical Midian. The tribe was always on the move, peripatetic. Guesses of modern scholars place the Midianites as far west as their trading in Egypt (remember the sale of Joseph?) and ranging east of the Jordan in the area of Moab, just near Mount Nebo. They no doubt grazed the lands in between, which includes the eastern edge of North Africa, northern portion of the Sinai peninsula, the Negev south of Beer Sheva and around Eilat, and finally, to the east of the Dead Sea. If we include incursions into the southern Sinai when scrub was scarce, Moses' Midianite shepherding led him to thoroughly scout what would be the route of the Israelites after the Exodus and up to their entry into the Promised Land.

Of course, for the sake of his own safety, Moses avoided the Egyptian Delta. There, the floodplains of the annual overflow of the Nile left rich, rich land. But at the edge of each year's flood limit, the North African terrain turned to scrubland. While sheep delighted in the thick grasses of the floodplain, they made do with the scrub. Shepherds marked their territories by cultivating cactus. The rows of impenetrable cactus kept sheep from making incursions into another shepherd's grazing turf and so made for good neighbors. These cacti also made for colorful borders across the horizon, Mickey Mouse–like heads and ears of cactus often festooned with climbers of bright red flowers. Shepherds were emphatically not welcome at the oases of date palms or among the interplanted groves of olive trees. No melons or garlic or leeks were allowed to the juggernaut of grazing sheep.

The Sinai was also scrub, but the terrain was far less flat. Oases and olive groves were few and far between. Instead, shade was offered by low acacia trees and the late-day shadows of the mountains. Shepherding among the wadis of the Sinai had its terrors when the rare rains brought flash floods hurtling down these wilderness ravines. In today's Sinai, bedouin herders mark their territory by hanging markers in the stubby trees, their tents often miles away, many wadis distant. To the untrained eye these markers are the road signs of the intertwining gorges of the wilderness.

Despite the looming presence of the Dead Sea, its sulfurous stench discernible from miles away, the lands of the Negev and the eastern side of the Jordan are arable, far less rocky than the Sinai. The rains are not much more plentiful, but they fill the plains of the rift valley with grassland. Here is the shepherd's delight. Even upward into the mountains of Moab there is good grazing. After the winter rains, this center of Midianite culture near Nebo and Madeba is a pastoral pleasure.

A good shepherd knows every inch of the lands his sheep graze. Moses was getting an excellent geography lesson in preparation for a mission he mulled as he shepherded his father-in-law's flock. Although we saw earlier that rabbinic tradition assigns a twenty- or forty-year span to this period of time, the biblical text so far gives us only the clues that Moses has married and borne a child, so we must imagine a period of two to forty years have passed during which Moses roams the wilderness, scouting the land, tending his father-in-law's sheep, and thinking about his people Israel, enslaved in Egypt.

The very people who rejected his leadership call to him in his mind to leave the father-in-law who has been so welcoming. Moses must weigh the pleasures of his newfound family and calling as shepherd against any return to Egypt. It is possible, even probable, that his birth family, the tribe of Levi, and the people Israel will still eschew his presence. And surely Moses has not forgotten that as much as he may be unwanted by the Israelites, he is very much on Egypt's most-wanted list. There were people who had wished to kill him, not least among them was his adoptive grandfather, the old Pharaoh, who had put the Israelites into slavery.

So Moses spends his days with the sheep, wondering what to do, what to do? With a burst of flame, his question finds an answer and his career as a shepherd is replaced by a higher calling:

> It came to pass after much time that the king of Egypt died. Yet the Israelites suffered from the enslavement and cried out. Their plea rose up to God and God remembered the covenant God made with Abraham, with Isaac and with Jacob. . . . Moses was shepherd of the

flocks of his father-in-law, Jethro, the priest of Midian. He had herded the sheep to the western wilderness where he came to the mountain of God, to Horev. A message from God came to him in a burst of flame from the midst of the bush. He looked and saw the bush engulfed in fire, yet the bush was not consumed!

Moses said, "I should turn aside and see this great sight. Why is the bush not burnt up?"

When God saw that Moses had turned aside to see, God called to him from the midst of the bush, God said, "Moses, Moses!"

He answered, "Here I am!"

God said, "Do not come near, but take your shoes off of your feet for the very spot you stand upon is holy ground."

God continued, "I am the Lord of your ancestors, the God of Abraham, the God of Isaac, and the God of Jacob." Moses hid his face for he feared to gaze at the Lord.

God continued, "I have seen the affliction of my people who are in Egypt. . . . I will come down to save them from the hand of Egypt . . . and bring them up to . . . a land flowing with milk and honey, to the place of the Canaanite, the Hittite, and Amorite, the Perizzite, the Hivvite, and the Jebusite . . . now go, I am sending you to Pharaoh to take my people the Israelites out of Egypt."

Moses asked the Lord, "Who am I to go to Pharaoh? Can I bring the Israelites out of Egypt . . . ? I will go to the Israelites and tell them that the God of their ancestors has sent me to them and they will ask me, 'What is his name?' What shall I tell them?"

The Lord said to Moses, "I will be what I will be. Tell the Israelites that 'I Will Be sent me to you.' . . . Go gather the elders of Israel and tell them, 'God, the Lord of your ancestors has appeared to me,' tell them, 'I will lift you up from the affliction of Egypt.' . . . They will listen to your voice so that you and the elders of Israel may go to the king of Egypt . . . but I know that the king of Egypt will not permit you to go without a strong hand. So I will send forth my hand and strike Egypt with all my wonders . . . only after that will they send you forth . . . nor shall you go forth empty-handed. . . ."

But Moses replied to God and said, "They will not believe me, they will not listen to me, they will say, 'God did not appear to you.'"

So God said to him, "What is that in your hand?"

He said, "A staff."

God said, "Throw it to the ground." So he threw it to the ground and it became a snake from which Moses fled.

God said to Moses, "Reach out your hand and grab it by the tail." So he reached out his hand and grabbed it and it became a staff in his palm . . . then God said to him, "Please, put your hand in your cloak." So he put his hand in his cloak and when he brought it out again his hand was scaly white like snow! God said, "Put your hand back in your cloak." So he returned his hand to his cloak and when he brought it out it had returned to flesh. "Thus, if they do not believe you or listen to your voice on the first sign, they will believe your voice on the latter sign. And if they do not believe these two signs and will not obey you, take some of the water of the Nile and it will turn to blood on the dry shore."

But Moses said to God, "Please, my Lord, I am not a man of words neither today nor yesterday, nor from the time you spoke to your slave; for I am heavy-mouthed and heavy-tongued am I."

God said to him, "Who placed a mouth on humans? Who makes one dumb or deaf, sighted or blind? Is it not I, God? Now go, for I will be with your mouth and instruct you what to say."

But he said, "Please, my Lord, send someone else."

God got angry with Moses and said to him, "Is not your brother Aaron the Levite? I know that he speaks well, so he will come to meet you and see you and be happy in his heart. You will speak to him and tell him what to say, I will be with your mouth and with his mouth. I will instruct you what to do. . . . Now take this staff in your hand, the one that you did the signs with."

So Moses went; he returned to his father-in-law, Jethro, and told him, "I wish to go, to return to my brethren in Egypt and see if they yet live."

Jethro said to Moses, "Go in peace."

God said to Moses in Midian, "Go, return to Egypt, for the men who sought your life have died."

Then Moses took his wife and his sons, he rode them on the donkey. Moses returned to Egypt with the staff of the Lord in his hand. (Exod. 2:23–4:20)

One last note on geography before we turn to destiny. In the south-central Sinai peninsula, the monastery of St. Catherine is still flourishing. There the monks tend to the oldest continually used library in the Western world. The fortresslike monastery sits at the foot of what the locals call Jebel Musa—in English: Mount Moses, a.k.a. Mount Sinai or Horev. It is fitting that this place is dedicated to the copying and preservation of books, located at the very spot where The Book was received by Moses. Just outside the library one can still see the carefully tended rosebush, aflame with bright red flowers blooming amid the thorns. The monks who tend it and keep it budding in the desert will solemnly tell curious tourists that this very bush is the same one God used to attract Moses' attention that fateful day some three millennia ago.

Yet as the story is told in Exodus, we readers and listeners are attended to before Moses is lured by the curiosity of a burning bush. At the very outset of the long narrative of God's epiphany to call Moses to lead the Jews from slavery, we are informed of a fact Moses himself would dearly like to know. "It came to pass after much time that the king of Egypt died," we are told. It is testimony to the narrator's art that this fact is withheld from Moses until he has taken leave of his father-in-law to set out on his journey back to Egypt.

It is testimony, too, to Moses' character that throughout the conversation with God, through all his demurrals and doubts about his own ability to lead and the Israelites' willingness to believe or follow him, not once does Moses query God regarding this most pressing fact. Surely it cannot have escaped Moses that his return to Egypt presents a personal risk. Having escaped Pharaoh's wrath, Moses is now required by God to return to Egypt and confront him once more. It is not clear whether Moses realizes that this is a new Pharaoh, not the grandfather who raised him. It is clear, however, that Moses' restraint in querying God about this personal issue is a remarkable sign of his legendary humility and his extraordinary qualification for the role he is about to play.

As for Pharaoh, we see a leader with new opportunities. He could have changed his predecessor's policies, emancipated his slaves, gone easy on the Israelites—but he has not. This is a Pharaoh who not only "knows not Joseph," but, as we will see, he refuses also to know God. His hubris results in a continuation of oppression. The continued oppression results in God remembering the covenant with Moses' and the Israelites' biblical ancestors. With memory comes action. This time is ripe for God to deliver the Jews. As the countdown to redemption reaches zero, there is ignition—the bush bursts into flame.

Moses' notice is compelled as surely as though he had witnessed a launch from Cape Canaveral. But the reverence that we feel when we watch a rocket launch is a curious blend of awe at the cosmos and pride in the human achievement evidenced as the booster hurtles its payload into the very heavens. With Moses the mix is purer, more rarefied. Surely there is awe in the stunning victory over nature as the bush burns without being consumed. But there is an unmistakable sense of the numinous as Moses responds to the voice of the One Who Spoke and so brought the very cosmos into being. The recognition of ineffable presence is a central part of the ultimate success of Moses' mission and one that we, no more than he, can afford to ignore. When the voice twice calls out his name, he responds as did his noble ancestors Abraham (Genesis 22:1) and Jacob (Genesis, 46:2), "*Hineni,* here I am."

This is not the place to discuss the extensive theology raised by God's revelation to Moses. The ancient and medieval rabbis cover every nuance of this conversation, beginning with the recognition that it takes place at Sinai, accompanied by fire, much as will the giving of the Ten Commandments upon Moses' return to the mountain following the deliverance from Egypt. As then, God begins with the identification, "I am the Lord . . ." At the giving of the Torah at Sinai, God speaks and Moses repeats God's words. Here, however, it seems that God speaks and Moses counters each of God's pronouncements with qualifications or doubts. It is the nature of this pas de deux that intrigues me. Like father Abraham pleading for ten righteous men of Sodom, Moses may not argue on his own behalf, but will risk haggling to assure the best possible deal for his extended family and for God's reputation.

God is not passive in this interchange. God baits Moses with tidbits, mixing the simple and wonderful with the complex and difficult. Moses is promised that the Israelites will inherit "a land flowing with milk and honey," a sweet lure if ever there was one. The shepherd Moses understands that a land flowing with milk means a land with rich enough pasturage to support huge flocks of goats—the principal source of the curds that are the Bible's "milk" in this passage. Abundance of flocks and pasturage will be complemented with fertile oases. The "honey" of this passage is not what bees make, but the gooey sticky stuff that coats the outside of dates. What Moses and the Israelites are promised is grazing land and palm trees. That's the good news.

God coats the bad news with the promise of abundant and prime real estate. But when Moses is informed that the lands being promised are the lands of the Canaanites, Hittites, Amorites, Perizzites, Hivvites, and Jebusites, the news is bittersweet. Yes, Canaan is the ancestral land promised to Abraham, Isaac, and Jacob. But six nations (and more) will need to be displaced in order to inherit the Promised Land. No safe harbor will simply be provided.

For the careful reader, the news is being broken to Moses that the conquest of the Holy Land will be a long time coming, and a difficult military achievement. Surely Moses himself understood this as he heard the litany of nations that had to be displaced. Moses knew that freedom from slavery was a long road, one that only began with exodus from Egypt. Perhaps, many years later, as he stood atop Nebo, Moses was relieved that his part of the journey was over. The dirty work of conquest and displacement would be given over to Joshua and the next generation. Moses could die with his hands clean, having accomplished his mission without uprooting whole families and tribes from their ancestral homes. Again, we see that the Torah is a book of the diaspora, unsullied by the nitty-gritty of territorial conquest.

It is almost as though this realization instills doubt and demurral in Moses. He asks, "Who am I to go to Pharaoh," wondering with this modest question whether he is up to the complex negotiations and moral decisions the task requires. With "who am I" comes a terror that he may not succeed. Further, Moses recalls only too well how his last foray into the "real world" of Egypt left him and the Israelites further at risk. He is aware that his very people may have similarly long memories and not be in the least interested in his erstwhile leadership. There is no question but that they will question his bona fides. If only the Israelites and Pharaoh could be given to understand that the mission was not that of Moses, but of God.

Thus Moses comes to ask for God's name, a clear sign of the authenticity and power of his undertaking. But the rabbis of the Talmud lament this request as a lack of faith on Moses' part. They imagine God replying, "How often did I reveal Myself to Abraham, Isaac, and Jacob. Yet they never doubted my attributes nor asked for My name. Yet you ask for My name at the outset, next you will call the entire mission into question!" This perceptive recognition of Moses' doubt is seconded by yet another rabbinic comment that attributes far more than mere doubt to Moses at this juncture. With the recognition of the power that comes with the knowledge of God's name, the ancient rabbis of a fifth- or sixth-century midrash to the book of Leviticus comment,

> When Moses acted in good faith, God responded in good faith.
> When Moses acted in innocence, God responded innocently.
> Yet when Moses acted craftily, God responded craftily. When did Moses act craftily toward God? When he inquired, "I will go to the Israelites and tell them that the God of their ancestors has sent me to them and they will ask me, 'What is his name?' What shall I tell them?" God responded appropriately for the moment and replied, "I will be what I will be."

This is an extraordinary explanation of what is an otherwise perplexing passage. Theologians for millennia have puzzled over this bizarre name for God. The rabbis who attribute craftiness to Moses attribute equal diplomatic aplomb with God's almost cavalier reply. It is as though God teases Moses, withholding the very name that will give Moses both authentication and power. "Oh," God is made to reply, "I will be what I will be." It is almost, as it were, a Scarlett O'Hara reply.

But within that seemingly flighty response to Moses' urgent request is the sure knowledge that God will not be trifled with. Moses must go on this mission, willy-nilly. Pharaoh will be strong-armed by plagues; Israel will be wowed by signs and wonders. Along with the staff that becomes a serpent, the hand that flakes white, and the water that turns to blood, God dispenses a piece of good politics, "Go gather the elders of Israel." In the third century the rabbis applaud this advice by having God play the part of the old pol to Moses' tyro. "Moses," God tells him, "pay court to the elders of Israel, give them some respect." God might as well have said, "Don't ignore your power base. All politics is local." With the foresight that only an omniscient God can have, the votes are already counted. God knows how this story will turn out, even if Moses does not. It is as reassuring to the reader as exit polls on election night.

Moses is left with one final ploy to learn what he can from God in order to assure the success of the mission he is about to undertake. God sends him on his way with the charge, "Now go, for I will be with your mouth and instruct you what to say." This is the moment for maximum risk, which Moses takes. Whether the risk is for himself or for the Israelites is the subject of debate. But even as God charges him to go to Egypt and not worry, Moses responds, "Please, my Lord, send someone else." The temerity of this refusal is well represented by a midrash written in Bulgaria, of all places, nine hundred years ago. The midrash has God respond to Moses by saying, "All you wanted then was to ask My name and converse with Me all this time?! You could have refused Me at the outset. But you wait until now, after all of our activity together to say, 'send someone else'?!"

Other midrash gives Moses more credit, for either humility or politics (but, apparently, not both together). Some rabbis suggest that Moses refuses to go because he has an older brother, Aaron, who is more worthy of the mission. This explains, perhaps, why God introduces Aaron into the plot. Other rabbis suggest that Moses implores God not to send humans but instead angels to redeem Israel, for their collective honor merits more than human intervention. Of course, this leads readers to appreciate the subtlety of both the midrash and of Moses in it, for the implication is that God, not Moses, should be doing the redeeming here. This subtlety is not as outrageous as it seems, for in the end it *is* God and not Moses who acts as Redeemer. Indeed, in the rabbinic celebration of the exodus during the Passover seder, Moses remains unmentioned in deference to God's role.

The twelfth-century commentary on this passage links Moses' final demurral with God's refusal to allow Moses into the Promised Land. God tells Moses, "You want to spend all this time refusing Me? I'll clip your wings. The time will come when you will beg me to enter the Land of Israel. And I will listen to you, but in the end will say, No, I will 'send someone else,' just like you ask of me now." This reading makes God out to be a bit petulant and perhaps vindictive. But God's anger is recorded here in Scripture, so Moses' risk at refusing must be reckoned as a mixed success at best.

In the end, God articulates what Moses has kept mum, and in so doing perhaps displays divine understanding for the unspoken and perhaps unrecognized motivation behind Moses' reluctance to return to Egypt. Moses has already bid his father-in-law farewell, so it is clear to us and to God that he has, however reluctantly, accepted his mission to return to Egypt and try to free the Jews. Then, and only then, unbidden God informs Moses, "the men who sought your life have died." This assurance permits him to feel safe enough to bring his wife and children with him. He saddles the ass, mounts them, and off he goes to Egypt. Two final notes need consideration before we accompany Moses.

First, he now has two children, not just Gershom. A second son has been born. Not until Exodus chapter eighteen are we informed of the second child's name. Like Gershom, who was named because Moses felt himself "a stranger in a foreign land," the second son's name bears note. He is called Eliezer and we are told in Exodus 18:4, "the Lord of my ancestors is my help, and has saved me from the sword of Pharaoh." "The Lord is my help" translates nicely into Hebrew: Eliezer. It is a good omen of the road to come.

But there is a second omen, a sign given to Moses to carry with him throughout the remainder of his journey. It is the shepherd's staff he carries. In the Bible we first see it when Moses asks God for a sign and it is turned into a serpent. It may have been the murder weapon with which Moses struck down the Egyptian taskmaster when he first left Pharaoh's palace. And we will see it again, once more turning into a serpent, this time before Pharaoh and his courtiers. And again, when Moses lifts it to part the Reed Sea into dry land. In the passage before us it is mentioned twice. Once as the "staff you did the signs with," and again as the "staff of the Lord."

It is no wonder, then, that this staff becomes the object of folktale and legend. A ninth-century midrash makes it out to be a precursor to King Arthur's sword in the stone: Rabbi Levi said that this staff was created on the eve of the Sabbath in the very week that the universe itself was created. The staff was given to Adam in the Garden of Eden. He in turn bequeathed it to Enoch who gave it in his turn to Noah. Noah used it to shepherd the animals onto his ark and then bequeathed it to Abraham. Abraham gave it to Isaac who gave it to Jacob. Jacob brought it with him to Egypt where he gave it to his son, Joseph, viceroy of Egypt. When Joseph died his household was despoiled and the staff passed into the palace of Pharaoh.

Jethro was one of Pharaoh's courtiers and he saw the staff and the magic letters of God's sacred name inscribed upon it. He longed for the staff to be his own. When the opportunity arose he stole the staff from Pharaoh's palace and buried it in his own back garden. There, it took root and no one could approach it because of the power it exuded.

When Moses came to Jethro's household he saw the staff and read the letters inscribed upon it. Moses reached forth his hand and drew the staff forth from the ground. Jethro stared at Moses and said, "This one is he who will free the Israelites from Egypt." It was thus that Jethro gave Moses his daughter Tzipporah as a wife and left the service of Pharaoh.

This tall tale links the staff of Moses to cosmic destiny. It was created at the dawn of the universe, has magical powers, and predicts Moses' role as redeemer of Israel. Through the staff we are informed of an imaginative job history for Jethro and how it happened that this Midianite priest came to have Moses for a son-in-law. One thousand years ago, the staff of the Lord marked a moment of delicious fantasy in the mouths of Jewish fabulists. Yet in the hand of Moses, the staff of the Lord marked his transformation from a herder of sheep to the shepherd of the whole house of Israel.

BRIDEGROOM

OF

BLOOD

I t sounds like a horror movie that should have starred Lon Chaney or Bela Lugosi: *The Bridegroom of Blood.* It is too easy to imagine the nighttime revelation of danger, the bizarre secret ritual, the shy bride stunned to see her groom imperiled. Were I the film director I might even be tempted to set the scene in some gothic precursor to the Bates Motel. I suppose if it were more up to date and somewhat more romantic, it could be an Anne Rice novel.

As it is, the scene *is* set in a motel and there is nighttime danger, bizarre ritual, shy bride, groom at risk, the whole schmear. In an almost postmodern feminist twist (perhaps worthy of Anne Rice), the shy bride herself slashes away and, covered with blood, saves her husband and children. And we haven't even mentioned the repressed sexuality of the narrative. Is it any wonder the Bible is a best-seller?

The steamy story I refer to is found in Exodus almost immediately following upon Moses' taking up his staff to set off to Egypt. A three-verse introduction provides the bridge from God's charge to Moses to the Bridegroom of Blood tale. The story itself, another of those wonders of biblical brevity, is three verses more. So, sit back and listen to half-a-dozen verses of wonder.

> God said to Moses, "When you go to return to Egypt you will see that all the signs I have put at your disposal will be performed for Pharaoh. Yet I will harden his heart so he will not let the people go. You tell Pharaoh, 'Thus says God, "Israel is My firstborn." God says to you, "Send forth my child to serve Me."' But he will refuse to send them out. Thus tell him, 'I [the Lord] shall kill your firstborn child.'"
>
> On the road that night, at the rest-stop, God encountered him and sought to kill him! Tzipporah took a flint and cut her son's foreskin off. She touched it to his "legs" and said, "You are my bridegroom of blood." He withdrew from him and she then said, "A bridegroom of blood of circumcision."

Weird. Or as my colleague Bible professor Rabbi Stephen Garfinkel characterized it, "enigmatic." That second paragraph, Exodus 4:24–26 is just a doozy. Aside from Tzipporah and God, there is nothing but pronouns. We may assume Moses is involved, certainly one of his sons is—the baby gets circumcised with a flint. Ouch. On the other hand, if it is the uncircumcised child who is threatened by God, perhaps because he is uncircumcised, getting cut is better than getting killed.

Before we enter the permutations of plot in these three lines and then, further, try to wrest some meaning from this "enigmatic" set of verses, there is the matter of God's charge to Moses. Like a good don, God sends Moses to the opposition with a message to deliver. Israel is family. You mess with family, I'll kill your kid. God speaks a language that Pharaoh knows how to hear. God sends Moses with bald threats of murder.

The text is actually somewhat more subtle. There is more to the threat than mayhem. From God's perspective, Pharaoh has presumed way too much power. Pharaoh invades God's turf by claims of divinity. So God not only demands freedom for God's "firstborn," God will also deny Pharaoh an essential part of his human character, his free will. Pharaoh will be constrained to refuse God's request. There will be no choice here. Pharaoh will be so backed into a corner that all of Egypt will go, as it were, to the mattresses on this one.

The twelfth-century rabbis saw it somewhat similarly, they imagine God says, in effect, "You hurt My firstborn, I'll hurt your firstborn." Another midrash from the same era invokes the prophet Isaiah (46:10), where God exclaims, "I foretell the end from the beginning." Indeed, the sorry ending of Pharaoh's refusal to free the Jews is set out clearly from the start. The last of the plagues of Egypt, the slaying of the firstborn, is warned of before Moses even begins his mission.

Perhaps it is to underscore this threat of death to Pharaoh that God arranges the little display that night at the motel. Like a horse's head on the pillow, the message is conveyed that God is not to be trifled with. God threatens and then delivers. Since it is God's intention to deliver in more than one sense of the word, Moses' family is left shaken but intact, while Pharaoh will soon be decimated. But maybe the Bridegroom of Blood episode is a brutal reminder to Moses as he sets out that there is no more room for trying to wiggle out. Go, speak to Pharaoh, or you or your children will suffer.

This reading is, perhaps, a bit too crude. For while Pharaoh may require such a brutal message, we would expect God to be more delicate and Moses no longer in need of quite so stark a display. Presumably Moses' last refusal to God, his "send someone else," was resolved. Moses should be on board, no need to suffer these brutal presentations of power. But as my friend Stuart Klawans has pointed out, this engagement with Moses is similar to a wrestling match his ancestor Jacob once fought. Like Moses, Jacob had then been away from the family for a long stretch, had married, and was now returning. On the road he met a "man" who wrestled with him, wounded him, and then sent him off with a blessing. Here, too, Moses is returning with family in tow, wrestles with a night visitor, and, thanks to Tzipporah's intervention, carries on with his journey under the banner of the covenant of circumcision.

This still leaves us with the problem of exactly who it is that suffers in the encounter with God. The rabbis mostly lean to it being Moses who is threatened, but not for the reasons I have suggested above. They wonder if Moses had neglected to circumcise one of his sons, perhaps out of deference to his Midianite priest father-in-law. Other rabbis suggest that Moses was delaying circumcision because he thought that the trip to Egypt took precedence. Yet others suggest that the urgency of the trip to Egypt was itself the cause. Given God's command to go, Moses should not have tarried at a motel. That delay was what endangered him.

A similar array of reasons can be adduced for the view that it was Moses' son who was endangered. Which son? Who knows. I vote for Eliezer, since he is possibly newly born here and, thus, not yet circumcised. But even if Eliezer were uncircumcised, it could have been Gershom who was endangered. Whether it was Moses, Gershom, or Eliezer, it is clear that Tzipporah's quick understanding of what is required saves the day. She grabs a sharp flint and circumcises the (unnamed) boy. Then she takes the bloody foreskin she has cut and touches it to "his legs." I imagine here it is Moses who is threatened and what she touches are not quite his "legs." The word *legs* is often a euphemism in the Bible for genitals, and it seems to be so here. Touching the foreskin to Moses' own penis has the effect of emphasizing that covenant in the flesh. It is this reminder of the covenantal relationship that causes God to withdraw from endangerment of Moses.

A medieval manuscript has a very clever take on this moment. It suggests that Moses was threatened because his son was uncircumcised. That he might go to Egypt to redeem the Jews and run the risk of them hooting at him, "physician heal thyself!" was untenable. Moses could make no demands on the slaves until he had fulfilled God's demand for circumcision on his own kin first. The invocation of circumcision and the covenant with God it represents is a strong moment in the narrative. The blood of circumcision saves Moses and the Israelites at large. Many midrashim invoke the blood of circumcision as the very act that kept the Jews in covenant with

God during their long slavery. It was observance of that one commandment that merited their redemption.

It also presages the blood of the Egyptians that will be spilled in the contest between God and Pharaoh. The Bridegroom of Blood incident shows us both the harrowing of the Jews and the destruction of the Egyptians that yet must take place before the exodus can occur. The stage has been set by this strange tale. Now his brother Aaron can enter the scene and together he and Moses can take on Pharaoh.

On a personal level, this bizarre tale shows us the struggles any leader and his or her family engages in as they set out on the path. Preparation for a protracted struggle with an opponent often requires some internal struggle, as well. Sometimes it is internal discord as the issues are clarified. Other times the family itself undergoes some transformative experience. Husbands and wives may clash. Children may, indeed, suffer. The heroism of leaders often comes at a cost to family. It is best to reckon that cost before it must be paid by those who may be unwilling to incur it.

As Moses returns to Egypt to face his past and take up his future with the Jewish people, it behooves Tzipporah to see the dangers that lie ahead. It may well be she and her children who are endangered by Moses' fulfillment of God's mission for him. When she takes the flint in hand, Tzipporah acknowledges the power of the covenant. As it were, she marries Moses again at that moment, this time with the Israelite covenant of circumcision and all the dangers it may hold. The blood of circumcision will cause yet more blood to be spilled—of Jews and of Egyptians both. Tzipporah understands this clearly when she declares Moses her "bridegroom of blood of circumcision."

We should pause a moment to marvel at Tzipporah. She is a Midianite woman, not an Israelite. Thus far she has been meek. Unable to withstand the shepherds, she had looked to Moses for succor. Relating the events to her father, she was chided for not taking the initiative to invite Moses home. Given to Moses in marriage, it appears that she passively acquiesces and equally passively bears him offspring. Yet the moment he or her child is threatened, Tzipporah jumps into the breach to take on God. She makes a choice for active involvement with full knowledge of the terrible stakes. Flint in hand she circumcises the boy and twice defiantly declares, "You are my bridegroom of blood . . . a bridegroom of blood of circumcision."

With this battle cry, Tzipporah joins the growing list of active female heroines in Exodus. There are the midwives who defy Pharaoh. There is Miriam, who protects her baby brother and goes on to assure his survival at her mother's bosom. There is the mother, Yocheved, who keeps the baby alive, afloat, satiated with her milk and wisdom. There is Pharaoh's daughter, who also defies her father and plays the role of stepmother to Moses. In the midst of a very male narrative, replete with foreskins, penises, blood, and threat to life, Tzipporah acts decisively to save Moses and, with him, perhaps, the future of Israel. The biblical book of Exodus displays a keen consciousness of the enormity of women's roles in keeping the people of Israel alive. Later rabbis will marvel at how these slave women gave heart to their husbands suffering under the crack of the taskmaster's whip. But the Bible itself leads the way, clearly recognizing women not merely as wives and mothers but as partners in affecting the redemption of the Jews.

The equality of women established through this three-verse horror film, the Bridegroom of Blood episode, draws to a close. Moses' big brother, Aaron, now enters the scene for the first time. The buddy action flick commences.

> God said to Aaron, "Go, meet Moses in the wilderness." So he went and encountered him at the mountain of God. He kissed him. So Moses told Aaron all the words of God who had sent him and about all the signs that God commanded. Then Moses and Aaron went and gathered together all the elders of the Israelites. Aaron spoke of all the things that God had told Moses. He performed the signs before the people. And the people believed and understood that God had remembered the Israelites and that God saw their misery. They bowed down and worshiped.
>
> After that Moses and Aaron came to tell Pharaoh, "Thus says God, Lord of Israel: Send forth My people, that they may celebrate a festival to Me in the wilderness."
>
> But Pharaoh replied, "Who is this 'God' that I should obey him and send forth Israel? I do not know God, nor will I send forth

Israel. . . . Why then, Moses and Aaron, do you seek to free the people from their tasks?"

That same day Pharaoh commanded the taskmasters and the capos among the people, saying: "Do not continue to provide straw to the people to make their bricks, as has been done in the past. Let them go themselves and gather straw. But do not lower the quota of bricks you require from what they have produced in the past. They are lazy. That is why they cry, 'Let us go make offerings to our Lord.'"

. . . So the taskmasters pressured them, saying: "Complete your daily workload as though you had straw!"

. . . The Israelite capos confronted Moses and Aaron. They gathered to encounter them when they came out from meeting with Pharaoh. They said, "May God look at you and judge you. You have made us stink to Pharaoh and his servants. You've put a sword in their hands to kill us!"

Then Moses returned to God and said, "My Lord, why have you made it so bad for this people? Why did you send me? Since I came to Pharaoh to speak in Your name, he has done bad to them. You have not saved Your people!"

God said to Moses, "Now you will see what I'll do to Pharaoh. He will send them out, strong-armed. Because of a strong arm he will drive them away from his land! . . . so tell the Israelites: 'I am God, I will take you out from under Egypt's burdens, I will save you from your slavery, I will redeem you with an arm stretched forth, with harsh judgments. I will take you as My people and I will be your God. Thus will you know that I am God, your Lord, who takes you out from under Egypt's burdens. . . .'"

So Moses told this to the Israelites, but they would not listen to Moses, for they were impatient due to the hard slavery.

Then God told Moses, "Come, speak to Pharaoh, king of Egypt, so he will send the Israelites out of his land."

But Moses replied to God, "Well, the Israelites did not listen to me, so how will Pharaoh listen to me, since I have uncircumcised lips?"

. . . So God told Moses, "Look here, I will make you a lord to Pharaoh, and your brother Aaron will be your prophet. You just say everything I command you and your brother Aaron will tell it to Pharaoh so that he will send the Israelites out of his land. I will harden Pharaoh's heart, until My signs and wonders will multiply in Egypt. Then Pharaoh will not listen to you, so I can set My hand upon Egypt and bring forth My host, My people the Israelites, with harsh judgments against the land of Egypt. Then will Egypt know that I am God, when I stretch forth My hand against Egypt and bring forth the Israelites from their midst."

Moses and Aaron did that which God commanded them. At the time they spoke to Pharaoh, Moses was eighty years old and Aaron was eighty-three. (Exod. 4:27–7:7)

If Tzipporah was the heroine of the first part of this chapter, she disappears as we get to Egypt and the confrontation with Pharaoh. It is as though the Bible, prefeminist document that it is, wishes to spare the ladies the discomfort of men going head to head. That this is wholly a boys' club is signaled by the arrival of Aaron. He and Moses manage to find one another in the wilderness, we assume with a little help from God. Indeed, Exodus is silent on just how Aaron can leisurely amble away from slavery to greet his brother at the mountain. Let it suffice that we may invoke either miracle or "the willing suspension of disbelief" to account for the brothers' reunion.

In one of the earliest commentaries the rabbis collected on the Bible, the scene is pictured with wit and imagination. The second-century rabbis have Aaron and Moses greet with hugs and kisses. Aaron asks his brother, "Moses, where have you been all these years?"

To which Moses responds, "Midian."

Aaron then asks the obvious, "And who are this woman and children with you?"

Moses answers, "The wife and kids."

"Where are you taking them?"

"To Egypt."

At that point in the rabbinic story, Aaron loses his cool. He has refrained from rebuking Moses for being away all this time. He does not chide him for not informing the family of his marriage or the birth of his children. The rabbis resist making Aaron into a whining elder sibling who complains, you don't call, you don't write, you don't fax ..., but they do have Aaron worry about the safety of his little brother's family, and, in so doing, solve a problem of biblical narrative.

Aaron said to Moses, "We are so worried about those already in Egypt, and you want to bring your family!?" At that moment, say the rabbis, Tzipporah returned to her father's house with the children. She waited with them there, out of harm's way, until the Exodus was completed, and only then joined Moses at his return to Mount Sinai. Thus is it written in Exodus 18, "Then Jethro, Moses' father-in-law, took Tzipporah, Moses' wife and her two sons, after she had been sent away . . . and came to Moses in the wilderness where he camped before the mountain of God" (Exod. 18:2–5).

The woman having been dispatched, the brothers can now turn their attention to attempting to dispatch Pharaoh and free the Jews. As instructed, they gather the elders of the Israelites who, for a change, are impressed with what Moses has to show them. They believe. They bow in worship. But not for long. By the time Moses and Aaron get their audience with Pharaoh, the elders, too, have vanished. This captures the rabbis' attention. Our twelfth-century source imagines the elders peeling off by ones and twos from the gang surrounding Aaron and Moses, so that by the time the troop arrives at Pharaoh's palace, the two brothers stand alone.

A thirteenth-century Yemenite midrash draws a more baroque picture of the elders' going AWOL. The gruesome imagery seems appropriate for the movie *Apocalypse Now,* with Moses and Aaron entering the heart of darkness. As Rabbi Eliezer tells it: "As they neared Pharaoh's palace the gates appeared as though they were a boiling cauldron. On one side were executed corpses, another route had crucified corpses, yet another had those whose hands or legs had been chopped off. Human beings were being stomped into the mud. When the elders saw this, they fled, thinking: better slavery than seeing this!"

Thus the scene is set for the first confrontation between Moses, Aaron, and Pharaoh. It is not a happy scene, either. Pharaoh displays remarkable arrogance. "Who is this 'God' that I should obey him and send forth Israel? I do not know God, nor will I send forth Israel." Ironically, Pharaoh's opening salvo, so full of bravado, seals his death sentence. In denying knowledge of God, much like his predecessor denied knowledge of Joseph, he calls down divine wrath. Pharaoh, who claims to be a creator-god, "The Nile is mine, I have created it!" (Ezek. 29:3), will be utterly smashed by the Creator of the Universe. Pharaoh either mistakes Aaron and Moses' mission for one of posturing—they do not really have divine power behind them—or, worse, thinks he can take on God. His dismissal of Moses and Aaron and subsequent intensification of oppression of the Israelites is a Pyrrhic victory. His brash challenge will be brief and result in enormous cost to all of Egypt.

Moses and Aaron leave disheartened. Their woe is exacerbated by the Israelites, who now suffer more than ever at the hand of their taskmasters. Having been seduced into producing a high quota of bricks, the commentaries suggest, the imposition of straw collection while still meeting the quota proved impossible. They lash out at Moses, who, they feel, has only increased their suffering. "May God look at you and judge you. You have made us stink to Pharaoh and his servants. You've put a sword in their hands to kill us!"

They again reject Moses' leadership. He does not see their despair, which the Bible adroitly accounts to the exhausted impatience that comes with hard labor. Instead, Moses accepts the possibility of his own failure at a task he was unsure of from the outset.

Moses turns the Israelites' anger directly back to God. He lashes out, "Why have you made it so bad for this people? Why did you send me? Since I came to Pharaoh to speak in Your name, he has done bad to them." A midrash composed about a thousand years ago imagines Moses backing away at this point. It is as though he tells God, "You wanted me to tell Pharaoh to free the Jews, I've done so. Now look what happened. I've done my job. Bye." Others see Moses' doubt of God as a clear sign of Moses' own despair and self-doubt. The text itself underscores this reaction to first failure. Moses actually reasons: If Israel will not listen to me, how can I expect Pharaoh to listen?

The last time Moses saw Israelites oppressed, he lashed out, killed an Egyptian, and then fled for his own life. His long exile has not increased his confidence in this situation. Pharaoh plays hardball and Moses may not yet be ready for the majors. Even with Aaron at his side, with God's staff in his hand, with God's directions leading him, Moses demurs. At the burning bush he had said, "send someone else." Now he compounds it and tells God, "You have not saved Your people!"

But God plays hardball with Pharaoh and with Moses. A second-century commentary on this passage has God sending him right back with a rebuke, "My children are mired in troubles while you stand here in comfort telling Me, 'send someone else'?!" Oh no, Moses will not be let off the hook that easily, nor can Pharaoh be left unpunished. Of course there will be opposition from him. It is inevitable that a power who is prepared to enslave a people will not simply roll over and play dead. Quite the contrary, Pharaoh must resist and then he must be punished. First for the enslavement and then for the resistance. Thus are tyrants broken and peoples freed from tyranny.

It is a hard lesson for meek Moses to learn. Moses desperately wishes that someone else will take up the cudgel. He has doubted that the Israelites will listen to him, he has worried he cannot speak well, he has inferred that Pharaoh will pay him no mind, he has even gone so far as to doubt God's saving ability. God loses patience with so much protest. It is no longer tolerated. Indeed, the next time God addresses Moses, our twelfth-century commentary points out, it is a joint address to Moses and Aaron. The midrash takes this as a rebuke to Moses, he no longer is the singular vehicle of revelation.

It could, however, be a lessening of Moses' burden, a palliative for his repeated requests to send someone else. God tells Moses, in effect, "Fine, now you and your brother will really do this together." Either way, it is a shift that enables Moses to return and confront Pharaoh yet again. Leadership cannot always be carried alone. Failure can be a cause for despair, but it can also lead to shared responsibility. Moses seeks someone he can trust, his brother, to carry on the fight when he has temporarily lost the confidence of the Israelites.

At the heroic age of eighty, Moses will reenter Pharaoh's presence to join the battle in earnest. The bargaining between them has high stakes. Moses cannot give in, for to do so is to fail both God and his people Israel. Moses recognizes that the slavery is so severe it is the very lives of his people for which he fights. And he surely recognizes that their lives may come at the cost of Egyptian lives. This, however, depends on Pharaoh and his devotion to the Egyptians. As with all tyrants in history, Pharaoh cannot see beyond himself. He will risk his country, his people, even his own son for the sake of his throne and his arrogance. In the end, it is Pharaoh who is the bridegroom of blood, but he is a bridegroom of blood with no recourse to covenant.

THE
PISSING
MATCH

I t is said that Passover is the most widely celebrated holiday in the Jewish community. This is not surprising. What's not to like about sitting around the table surrounded by family and loved ones, eating, eating, and then eating some more, while acknowledging the double blessings of ancestry and freedom? Some of my fondest childhood memories are set at the Passover seder table, where my grandfather, father, aunts, and uncles raced through the Hebrew ritual with a glee that I otherwise rarely saw. They sang, they ate, they argued and laughed. And, of course, there was wine, lots of wine. The seder—the ordered ritual to celebrate Passover—requires that each participant, even the pauper eating with public assistance, have no less than four cups of wine. As the Psalmist observes, "Wine gladdens the human heart."

The wine drinking itself is subject to its own ritual, with blessings before and afterward—toasts to God who created wine, to the holiday, and to God who caused it. But one of the most curious rituals of the seder involves spilling wine. Now, I know this happens at practically every dinner party, but at the seder the spilling of wine is no accident. Each participant consciously spills out ten drops of wine as those assembled recite the list of the ten plagues brought against Pharaoh and Egypt. Some folks dip their pinky into the cup and drip out one drop at a time. In Hebrew they (re)count: *dam* (blood), *tzefarde'ah* (frogs), *kinnim* (lice), *arov* (wild beasts), *dever* (pestilence), *shekhin* (boils), *barad* (hail), *arbeh* (locusts), *khoshekh* (darkness), *maqqat bekhorot* (killing the Egyptian firstborn). For every plague a drop of wine. My cousin, the surgeon, is more germ conscious; he uses a glass cocktail stirrer to remove his wine drops. Others use a spoon or the back of a fork. Then there are those, terrors of hosts and hostesses everywhere, who simply spill their wine over the side of the cup.

I am often asked why it is that we spill wine out of our cups at the seder. I answer honestly that I do not know. I don't. But I do have some theories and I will offer three here in order of increasing likelihood. The first invokes an oft-cited midrash that has God rebuke the angels who wish to sing God's praises when the Israelites are saved and the Egyptians are drowned in the Reed Sea. God rebukes them: "My creatures are drowning and you wish to sing!" This lovely midrash recognizes that if God is the creator of the universe, the creator of humanity in God's own image, then both sides of a conflict have God on their side. When one party loses, is harmed, God has sympathy for them; even as God may delight for the winners. This being the case, in an act of *imitatio dei,* we, too, show our sorrow for the Egyptians who drowned, by lessening our glasses a mite for each plague they suffered.

I love this explanation since it oozes liberal sympathy for our enemies. But, frankly, I doubt that it has any historic heft to it. Passover is a night when Egypt is the undeniable heavy; when Jews quote Psalms, "Pour out Your wrath on those who do not know You," and recommend that God fulfill the verse of Lamentations, "Pursue them in fury, obliterate them from under the very heavens." I am dubious that the ten drops of wine could be meant as a sympathetic gesture in the midst of all that fury.

I am far more inclined to seek the origins of the gesture in the origins of the seder ritual itself: the Greco-Roman symposium banquet or cocktail party (my cousin's swizzle stick already makes more sense). Throughout the antique world in which the rabbis lived, the symposium was the dinner party par excellence. When faced with choosing a format for their own seder, the rabbis went with the symposium, for it combined celebration with literary pretension. Since the seder mixed freedom and wine with readings from Scripture, the symposium was an excellent model. It was also the ancient world's black-tie dinner. But the Greeks who partied at symposia were pagans, and it was their custom to pour libations to the gods before drinking wine. "To Bacchus!" they would toast, or "To Zeus, the Savior!" Now, such idolatrous libations—actual pouring out a few drops of wine onto the dirt floor before imbibing—simply would not do at a Jewish celebration. The seder was solemn ritual, Jewish to the core. This pagan custom of pouring out wine needed some circumcising, as it were. The custom itself was virtually impossible to eradicate, social etiquette being what it was. So some rabbi got the idea of continuing it but invoking the ten plagues as the cause for all the pouring (remember "pour out Your wrath . . ."?). I am still dubious, chiefly because I think the rabbis would have worked hard to eradicate the libation, which was idolatry, in its entirety, rather than recast it.

My third suggestion also stems from the symposium banquet and also relates to social custom in the hellenistic world. It is important to remember that although I have characterized the symposium as a black-tie cocktail party, it does not necessarily share all of the same conventions as our own events. Symposia were the standard dinner-party format in the ancient world for hundreds and hundreds of years. We have literature of the symposium dating as early as Plato and as late as the fifth century of the common era. Throughout this literature reference is made to a raucous table custom called *cottabos*. Actually, it was a game, played by balancing a thin silver plate on a tall cylinder. The stakes of the game varied—the winner getting anything from kisses, to food, to the right to carry home the centerpiece.

The object of the game was to knock the silver plate off of its perch. This was accomplished by taking the last few drops of wine in a cup and, with a flick of the wrist, spinning them out of the cup and at the plate. The first one to knock the plate off (with much ensuing clatter) wins! I feel secure the game of *cottabos* is behind our own splashing of wine. Again, the rabbis took a hellenistic custom and Judaized it, possibly making it somewhat tidier than it had been originally. Much depends on how the wine gets spilled as the ten plagues are recited.

That the plagues occupy a central place in the Passover seder is not surprising, for they cover a major portion of the narrative in Exodus. Four full chapters of the Bible (one tenth of Exodus' forty chapters) are given over to an account of the first nine plagues. What is lacking in the seder, but very present in the biblical account, is Moses. This is not mere coincidence. Most scholars assume, absent any explicit testimony, that the ancient rabbis who devised the seder worried about giving Moses pride of place at the seder table. Passover and its ritual are celebration of God's redemption, not Moses' triumph. So at the seder table, Moses is passed over in silence.

But in the biblical account in Exodus, Moses' growth and development as a leader is charted with every passing plague. His clash with Pharaoh is diagrammed in detail. The first nine plagues are certainly accounts of God's miracles as plagues roll in on Egypt to decimate the land and Pharaoh's will to keep the Jews enslaved. But the human interest story is that of Moses and his increased confidence and ability to bargain for the freedom of the Jews and all that is theirs. In the strains of battle with Pharaoh, Moses becomes the great leader as he is known by subsequent generations. In the same battle, Pharaoh declines in prestige until his pretensions not only to godhood but even to national leadership are exposed as hollow. With God above and Aaron at his side, Moses takes on Pharaoh in a match of epic proportions. As we review the Exodus account we will focus on Moses' growth, his bargaining gambits, and his insistence that the redemption of the Jews is not only about freedom but an absolute acknowledgment of God's sovereignty.

This is aptly characterized by a thirteenth-century Spanish preacher named Rabbi Shimeon. At the outset of the contest between Moses and Pharaoh, God instructs Moses to have Aaron take his staff and throw it to the ground that it may become a

ent, as a sign to Pharaoh. As it happens, Pharaoh's court magi-
ans reproduce the trick themselves, but then Moses' staff swallows
up the serpents produced by the Egyptians. Rabbi Shimeon explains:
The Blessed Holy One said that this evil Pharaoh boasts and calls
himself a serpent—as it says in the prophet Ezekiel (29:3) of
Pharaoh, "Great serpent who sprawls in his Nile saying, 'The Nile is
mine, I have created it'" —go now, Moses, and tell him, "Do you see,
this staff made of dry wood has become a serpent that swallows up
all of your serpents. But in the end, it will return to being dry wood.
But as for you, Pharaoh, I created you from a putrid drop of sperm
and given you kingship. Yet you commit hubris and claim to have
created the Nile. Behold, I will reduce you to primeval chaos! You
swallowed all the staffs of the tribes of Israel, I will force you to
vomit them up. I shall bring ten plagues upon you on behalf of
Israel!"

The instructions in the Bible to Moses to take on Pharaoh are
quite explicit, "Go to Pharaoh in the morning when he goes out to
water, stand forth and confront him at the shore of the Nile with the
staff that turned into the serpent in hand" (Exod. 7:15). If the phallic
symbolism of this *mano a mano* challenge are not clear enough, an
eleventh-century midrash makes it obvious by asking, "Why did
Pharaoh 'go out to water'? Because that evil man used to boast that
he was divine and did not have bodily needs. So he would sneak out
early every morning to attend to his 'water' before his subjects saw
him. This is why the Blessed Holy One sent Moses to the shore early,
to catch him making water." So Pharaoh is approached by Moses at
the shore of the Nile at a vulnerable moment. Moses carries the
staff/serpent in his hand just as Pharaoh takes his "serpent," as it
were, in his hand. Hence the title of this chapter.

The rabbis never tire of poking fun at this Pharaoh with his pretensions to divinity. They caricature him, paint him with dwarf proportions, despite his enormous ambitions. Well, almost dwarf, for in
their ribald humor they do match the outlandish size of his aspira-
tions. In the Talmud we read of a certain barber who reported that
"Pharaoh was but a cubit high and his beard was a cubit long. But
his schmuck was a cubit and a handsbreadth." This vulgar cartoon
of the enemy is the stuff of oppressed peoples everywhere. With
nothing more to strike back with, the wit of dirty jokes becomes the

weapon. Pharaoh is reduced to a Priapus, erect
unable to finish what he boasts.

This is not to say that Pharaoh is benign. He r
to recognize God and free the Israelite slaves. He toys
the negotiations and stands up to the plagues, no matter wh.
cost to the Egyptian people. In the end, of course, the plagues reach
his person and his tune changes. By then, Moses has felt his own
mastery of the situation and presses Pharaoh to give in entirely.

Pharaoh is obdurate. In each of the first five plagues the Bible
reports that Pharaoh hardened his heart and did not give in. For the
last five plagues, Exodus reports that God hardened Pharaoh's heart.
It is as though God strips Pharaoh not only of his pretensions to divinity but even of that which so clearly defines his humanity, his free will.
However, a Pharaoh lacking free will is nothing but a puppet. His
continued refusal to free the Jews becomes a theological question.
Could not God have freed the Jews all the sooner in that case?

Two third-century rabbis are reported discussing this very issue.
Rabbi Yochanan notes that the hardening of Pharaoh's heart by God
offers an opening to heretics to claim that there was no opportunity
for Pharaoh to repent. Yochanan's colleague and brother-in-law
Rabbi Shimeon ben Laqish shuts the door to this possibility. He
explains that when God warns a person once, twice, three times and
more, and the person still does not repent, then God locks up his
heart to any possibility of change in order to punish him for his sins.
In the case of Pharaoh, God sent him five opportunities to change
his mind, but he refused to attend to them. At that point, God determined to match Pharaoh obstinacy for obstinacy so that his punishment would be appropriately doubled.

This notion of warning before punishment is also noted in the
pattern of the plagues themselves. Already a millennium ago, but
again in this century in the enlightening commentaries on Exodus
by Professor Nahum Sarna, an order of the plagues is discerned.
The first nine plagues fall into three sets of three each (that is:
plagues 1–3, 4–6, 7–9). The first of each set has Moses going out to
challenge Pharaoh at his early morning toilet. There, Moses confronts Pharaoh, demands release of the Israelites, and makes explicit
the punishment to follow should Pharaoh refuse. When Pharaoh
refuses, plagues one, four, and seven follow in course. For the second

plague in each set of three, Moses again confronts Pharaoh (but not in the morning) and warns him of the consequences. Pharaoh's heart is hardened and he refuses to release the Jews. Plagues two, five, and eight follow.

The third plague in each set of three comes without warning. It is as though Pharaoh gets two strikes. Once he misses his opportunity, a third plague strikes without any interaction between Pharaoh and Moses. Plagues three, six, and nine devastate Egypt with no intervening dithering. By the third round of three, Pharaoh has utterly decayed. He is but holding on by a thread. Still, in his long practiced obstinacy and towering ego, he endures against Aaron, Moses, the Jews, and God. Indeed, by the outset of the eighth plague, Pharaoh's own courtiers have folded and he stands against them, too. They advised Pharaoh, "How long will this one [Moses] be a snare to us? Send these people forth . . . don't you know yet that Egypt is lost?" (Exod. 10:7).

The narrative of the plagues is rich in detail and structure. I will comment on one more feature of the structure, but for now I want to take a moment to treat one individual plague. I choose it as representative, any of the others carries its own drama and centuries of commentary. This selective reading may be a good opportunity to remind you to go read the biblical account. Exodus has fabulous riches to explore. This book in your hands is but one of many ways of reading the Bible, whether traditional-religious or secular-academic. The more you read, the more you will see. The more you study, the more you will learn. The more you argue out your positions and readings on the text of Exodus, the farther you will travel on your own road.

But for now, let's hop down the road a bit with frogs. Frogs have been a source of revulsion and fascination since they first shed their tails and climbed out of the primordial muck. Perhaps their very amphibious nature makes them the darling of folktales. For if they can change from fishlike creatures of the water to broad jumpers on land, perhaps they can change with a kiss into Prince Charming. For Egypt, there were neither kisses nor happy endings when the second plague, frogs, came upon them. Frogs swarmed the land, "they ascended from the Nile and came into the houses, into bedrooms, onto beds, into servant quarters, onto maids, into the ovens and onto the dough" (Exod. 7:28). Readers of the Bible and hearers of the legend long ago are meant to utter a collective "Ick!"

The midrash, of course, delights at this discomfiture of the enemy. But, typically, the entrée into the text comes with a peculiarity of biblical grammar. When Exodus reports the advent of the frogs, it uses a collective noun. In Hebrew, the text reads, *vata'al hatzefarde'ah,* which is a singular verb and noun. It could be translated, overliterally, "the frog arose," even though it is clear from the context that we should more properly render it as a plural, "the frogs arose." Enter the second-century Rabbi Aqiba, one of the most famous legalists of the rabbinic world and a purported founder of an entire school of biblical interpretation. Tongue, I suspect, in cheek, he comments, "There was but one frog. It spawned enough to fill all of Egypt." His colleagues, either unaware that the man had a sense of humor, or aware that he had none and was being all too literal, rejoined, "Aqiba, what business have you mucking about in biblical narrative? Stick to your legal expositions on the transmission of ritual unfitness. The proper interpretation," they tell him, "is there was one frog who rose up from the Nile. Then he whistled and his fellow froggies joined him."

If this display of interpretative legerdemain is not enough to capture the serious silliness with which ancient rabbis read these stories, consider a commentary from the mid-ninth century. "The frogs were everywhere. The Egyptians even heard them croaking in their bellies. What did they say? *kav lekav.* Not only that, but when an Egyptian would go to the outhouse in search of relief, a frog would jump out and bite him on his rectum. Nothing could be more embarrassing." As we might characterize this in the locker room: What a bite in the ass! But here, too, beyond its crude appeal, there is some wisdom. The froggy sounds erupting from Egyptian bellies carry meaning. In rabbinic Hebrew, *kav lekav* translates neatly as the fate of Egypt: "measure for measure."

Let us leave the frogs' croaks to echo in our ears a few moments as we return to the broader structure of the plagues. It has been noted for centuries now that the first three plagues are performed by Moses' brother, Aaron. Blood, frogs, and lice all come at Aaron's beckoning. The midrash even comments that it was not fitting for Moses to bring either blood or frogs, since each of those two plagues affected the Nile adversely. And it was the Nile that had saved Moses as a baby. Rather than have Moses smite the waters that saved him, the task was delegated to Aaron.

But I am more taken by an observation that divides the plagues into groups of three. The first three plagues do belong to Aaron. But it should be noted that three plagues are God's direct doing (wild beasts, pestilence, and killing the Egyptian firstborn). Three more are at Moses' hand (hail, locusts, and darkness). One other plague remains, and it—the plague of boils—was accomplished by the combined efforts of Moses, Aaron, and God. So, again, there is a three by three pattern with one more to round out the ten.

This structure is more than coincidental. It effectively outlines the rise in Moses' ability as a leader, as one who negotiates, even battles on Israel's behalf. The first three plagues, when Moses is least confident, are performed by his older brother. The next two are accomplished by God. The sixth plague, boils, invites Moses into the mix of actors who strike out against Egypt. Only then, with assurance that the enemy is already weakened, and in full confidence of his own powers, does Moses join the fray. He greets Pharaoh in the morning as he has before, but this time it is he who unleashes the plague that follows Pharaoh's refusal. When the courtiers buckle, Moses is emboldened. He knows them and their ilk from his youth. He warns Pharaoh once more. Pharaoh still refuses. Moses boldly unleashes the eighth plague, the destructive hoard of locusts that eat what little is left after the plague of fiery hail Moses has wreaked on Egypt. After Pharaoh again refuses, Moses follows the earlier pattern and at the wave of his hand brings total darkness upon Egypt. Pharaoh's power is eclipsed. Moses' moon shines bright in that darkness, reflecting the glory of his God.

Moses' actions allow God respite to play the role of good cop to Moses' bad cop. It does not suffice for God to merely destroy Egypt. The point of the plagues is for God to teach the Egyptians the futility of relying on the merely human power of a Pharaoh. With Pharaoh reduced to rubble, the Egyptians may see the error of their ways. Yet for them to turn to God requires an act of mercy and beneficence, even as the kingdom falls around them. Thus, as Moses brings down hail from the heavens, he reports God's offer of refuge to the common Egyptian, "Bring in your flocks and all you have in the field, every human and beast that have yet to be gathered indoors, lest the hail rain down upon them and they die" (Exod. 9:19).

Moses plays the dual role of enforcer and prophet. He delivers a religious message, belief in the one God, even as he destroys Pharaoh and frees the Jews. Once Moses has found his voice he is implacable. Following the ninth plague, Pharaoh offers a partial palliative, "Go serve God; leave but your sheep and cattle behind" (Exod. 10:24). Moses does not give an inch. In fact, he ups the ante and demands that Pharaoh himself provide flocks and cattle to offer as sacrifice to God. This serves a double purpose. It requires that Pharaoh be subservient and offer obeisance to God. Moses also rubs salt into the wound of Pharaoh's submission. He will not only lose his slave force, he will pay for the privilege.

As Moses articulates it in his initial demand to Pharaoh before he brought the plague of locusts upon Egypt, "Our children and our elders will go, our sons and our daughters, our sheep and our cattle, we will all go to celebrate the festival of God" (Exod. 10:9). And so it shall come to pass. Moses has been tested and proved as a leader. He will be tested yet again by Pharaoh and by the Jews. There is yet more drama before the Exodus can begin.

MIDNIGHT

The Five Books of Moses are most often studied in Jewish contexts with the commentary of Rashi. In fact, the standard method of printing a Hebrew Bible text is with Rashi's commentary running alongside, either with the accompaniment of an Aramaic translation or with an array of other commentaries, so that there is a multicenturied conversation on the printed page. As printer's art, the page is elegant, varying type sizes and typefaces seemingly offering clues to the importance of opinions or, perhaps, the geographical origins of the commentator. If it were an English page, we might see Gothic type set against italic or roman. In Hebrew typeface, the standard font carries the biblical Hebrew text center page; while below it runs the commentary in a typeface called, in his honor, Rashi.

*Ra*bbi *Sh*lomo *I*tzchaki, Solomon the son of Isaac, wrote his commentary in the eleventh century in the wine country of Troyes, in what is now France. He opens his famous commentary on the Torah at Genesis 1:1, "In the beginning." At this opening verse Rashi suggests, "The Torah should have begun at Exodus 12:1 . . ." This is, admittedly, a provocative, even peculiar start for a Torah commentary, especially *the* Torah commentary. To be fair, when he wrote, Rashi did not know that his comments would become the standard interpretation of the Torah for the next thousand years. Still, it gives pause to wonder what was so special about Exodus 12 that Rashi would have reordered the Torah so that all of the Genesis narrative and all the Exodus story we have read up to now should defer to it.

What is there seems at first blush to be a digression, an aside to the thrust of the biblical narrative. It is an interruption to the high drama of the last plague, the slaying of the Egyptian firstborn. This last plague finally breaks Pharaoh's will, and so directly results in the ensuing exodus. Why, then, does the Torah take a break just at the peak of the action to meander in a "by the way" rather than get on with the story? Now, it is a rule among narrators to slow down the action just at the plot's peak. In B-grade films, a director might resort to slow motion. In action novels, there may be an entire chapter devoted to subplot just when the reader is expecting to learn who done it. In great literature, the diversion often reveals the point of the novel in miniature. The side road parallels or intersects the plot in such a way that all is revealed to the perceptive reader in the moments before it is revealed to the characters in the book. In a way, that is what is going on in the narrative of Exodus. Just as the climax of the Egypt story is introduced, there is an aside full of rules about the sacrifice of the paschal lamb.

For Rashi, this is the whole point of the Torah. He has patiently waited while the narrative lumbered along to get to the real meat of the book—what the rabbis call *halakha,* often translated following the Greek convention as law *(nomos).* But for Rashi and his disciples, as well as for those who preceded and followed them, *halakha* was more aptly the "way to go," a prescription for life. The rules about the Passover sacrifice were the stuff rabbinic Jews lived for and by, the details wherein God could be found. In the ancient rabbinic community, *halakha* most often took pride of place over narrative. Oh yes, everyone needed stories, and the Torah and rabbinic literature were full of those. But what people really needed was direction, and *halakha* provided the right way to go. This was true in the nascent Christian community as well. The Acts of the Apostles speaks of *hay hodos,* The Way by which believing Christians should guide their lives. Even those dour sectarians at Khirbet Qumran, the folks who gave us the Dead Sea Scrolls, write of the *derekh* or Path to live by. Each of these three communities, all bound up with what they each saw as a life of Torah, took *hay hodos* or the *derekh* or followed *halakha* so that they could be traveling in the right direction on the road.

So when the Torah turns to ritual, rules, sacrifice, details of the law, Rashi feels at home. For him, Exodus 12 is not so much an interruption in the narrative as the whole point of the story. And the Torah itself underscores this centrality by doubling the rules given: once for the historic present of Egypt and again for all future generations to commemorate. That is to say, the enslaved Jews about to be freed are given certain rituals that are to serve them in one way or another during the exodus. At the same time, many of these rituals are prescribed for future Passovers to enable Jews to reenact the Exodus and remember their redemption.

This admixture of "narrative and *nomos*" (as the late Professor Robert Cover called it), the merging of legal or ritual prescription with national story, is perhaps the stylistic signature of the Torah from this point onward. From Exodus 12 through the very end of the Five Books, at Deuteronomy 34, the myth of Israelite origins and wanderings is intermingled with *halakha* much in the same way, say, that Herman Melville united whaling particulars with the tale of Ahab's obsession. It is not coincidence that Melville endowed the characters of *Moby Dick* with biblical names.

There is, of course, more to this combination of genres than mere narratology. A late medieval midrash links the advent of *halakha* to the narrative in a quite pragmatic fashion: "When Israel were in Egypt they were astonished, saying of themselves, 'We have no commandments whatsoever with which to occupy ourselves and thus gain merit to be redeemed.' As soon as God heard that, Moses was commanded to give them the laws of the paschal sacrifice. As Rabbi Yuda said, 'If we reckon the laws of the paschal sacrifice, they had credit for more than thirty commandments.'"

This pragmatism demands some explanation, since it would not do for readers to think that the rabbis, even late medieval rabbis, imagined such a direct causal nexus between performance of God's commandments and redemption. Without a doubt, rabbis encourage Jews to the observance of the commandments by underscoring the great rewards God gives for such obedience. But Israel's merit was such that God's intervention to free them from slavery was inevitable. I am particularly spelling this out to avoid any appearance of painting rabbinic Judaism as a form of "works righteousness," a phrase used to cheapen Judaism by German Protestant theologians of the last century who were intent on superseding Judaism. The works righteousness mentality can be construed as a system of Brownie points, each fulfilled commandment earning the Israelites credits in God's account book. To some extent, this, like all caricatures, is a reflection of both the Torah and its rabbinic interpreters. But it is a distorted reflection.

In their celebration of *halakha,* the rabbis would happily assent to the idea that God rewards behavior in accordance with the commandments. There are many midrash texts that speculate on what merits the Jews had earned to be redeemed. But the rabbis would be equally quick to point out (as is this rabbi) that the system is more complicated. Even without performance of commandments, even for sinners, God remembers the covenant and frees the oppressed. This aspect of God's grace is a universal message of Judaism, which does not reserve salvation for Jews alone. Jews have commandments to perform, true, but everyone is God's creature and thus worthy of redemption.

It should be clear to the reader that the very advent of *halakha* into the biblical narrative has revved me up to high gear. At this speed the sermons and attendant theology just come pouring forth. It is time to downshift to a more sedate speed and return to the story of Exodus. With the text as our map we are less likely to stray too far off the road.

God told Moses, "I will bring yet one more plague upon Pharaoh and Egypt. After that he will send you forth from this. He will drive you out in the end. So speak, please, to the people that they may borrow from their neighbors, men and women respectively, vessels of silver and vessels of gold."

God made the Egyptians look favorably upon the people. Furthermore, the man Moses was very great in the land of Egypt, in both the eyes of Pharaoh's servants and in the eyes of the people.

Moses said, "Thus God says, 'Around midnight I will go forth amid Egypt. Every firstborn of Egypt will die—from the firstborn of Pharaoh seated on his throne to the firstborn of the maidservant behind the mills, even the firstborn animals. There will be a great outcry throughout the land of Egypt, unlike any that has ever been or ever will be. But against the Israelites, whether human or beast, no dog will even scrape his tongue; that you may know that God distinguishes between Egypt and the Israelites. . . .'"

God spoke to Moses and Aaron in the land of Egypt saying, "This month shall be for you the first month of the year. Speak to the entire assembly of Israel saying, 'On the tenth day of this month let each man take a lamb for his family, one lamb per house . . . you shall guard it until the fourteenth day of this month, then all of the congregation of the assembly of Israel shall slaughter it at twilight. You shall take of the blood and put it on the two doorposts and upon the lintel, on those houses where you eat it. You shall eat the meat roasted on this night, together with matzo and bitters. . . . Thus shall you eat it: with girded hips and sandals on your feet, with walking stick in hand. . . .' I will pass through the land of Egypt on this night, and I will strike every firstborn in the land of Egypt, from man unto beast, I will wreak judgments upon all the gods of Egypt, I am God. And the blood will be a sign for you upon the houses where you are. I will see the blood and pass over you, so when I strike Egypt there will be no plague to destroy you.

"This day shall become a memorial for you, which you shall celebrate as a holiday of God for your generations. Celebrate it as an eternal institution. You shall eat matzo for seven days, but on the first day remove all leaven from your houses, from the first through the seventh day . . ."

So it happened that at midnight God struck every firstborn in the land of Egypt, from the firstborn of Pharaoh sitting on his throne to the firstborn of the captive imprisoned in the pit, even every firstborn animal. By night Pharaoh arose, he and all his servants and all Egypt; and there was a great cry in Egypt, for there was no house which did not have a corpse there. He called to Moses and to Aaron by night and said, "Arise! Go out from amid my people, both you and the Israelites, go serve your God as you have said!" (Exod. 11:1–12:31)

We are meant to hear the frantic tone in Pharaoh's capitulation. Had the plague of killing the firstborn only affected the captives in the pit, Pharaoh might well have hardened his heart yet again. But this time his own child dies as a result of his intransigence. There is, of course, a symmetry to the situation, a measure for measure inevitability. From the very outset of the narrative we have been waiting for this particular shoe to drop. While still standing at the Burning Bush, Moses was informed that Egypt would be despoiled. Vessels of silver and gold would be "borrowed," perhaps as the midrash would have it, in fair restitution for the many years of slavery.

When Moses set off with his wife and sons to return to Egypt, before he ever encountered this unknown Pharaoh who so rashly denied knowledge of God, indeed, just before Moses and Tzipporah encounter the night terror in the Bridegroom of Blood episode, it was then that Moses heard that Egypt's firstborn would be slain. It seems that this knowledge weighed heavily on Moses, remaining at the forefront of his consciousness as he carried out his mission. Perhaps Moses engaged in the give-and-take of the plagues in order to try to preclude this terrible death, one that he had witnessed among Israelites in his own childhood. Yet when the hour was nigh Moses did not need to have a direct command from God to tell Pharaoh what was coming. Once Moses heard that the Israelites were to despoil Egypt, he knew that the hour of death had also arrived.

And so, Moses prophesies to Pharaoh of the plague to come. He is careful not to forewarn Pharaoh too exactly, he temporizes, "Around midnight . . ." When God does bring the plague of death, there is cosmic precision. Exactly at midnight the blade falls. It falls on those who labor at the mills. It falls on those captive in the pit. It falls on the offspring of Pharaoh, seated no longer firmly upon his throne. And again, Israel is unscathed. In the piquant words of Exodus, "no dog will even scrape his tongue" against the Jews. It is a moment of stunning power for the once-stuttering Moses. His arch foe Pharaoh is wholly humbled before him. Indeed, God's promise has been fulfilled, Moses is like a god to Pharaoh, and Aaron is his prophet. "The man Moses was very great in the land of Egypt." At this moment of power, when not only Egyptians but even the Jews hold Moses in favor, he begins his transformation from general and liberator to leader and lawgiver.

This transformation will take some time yet, and the Israelites in particular will have a difficult time sustaining their faith in Moses and the God whom he represents. But at this moment, between the pronouncement of the plague to come and its midnight depredation, when the promise of redemption is palpable, Moses and Aaron are told to announce a new era, "this month shall be for you the first month of the year." The rules that follow mark a transformation not only for Moses but for the people Israel as well. Up until now, they had served Pharaoh. Their rules involved grueling physical labor: building, brick making, gathering straw. Every labor was done on a quota system. No mercy was shown to slackers.

Now, a new service is embarked upon. The people Israel serve God, restoring a covenantal relationship made with their ancestors before their descent into the slavery of Egypt. The labors they perform for God are ritual, celebratory. The Israelites are required to have a lamb roast, the leftovers are offered to God. The blood of the lamb is dipped with a hyssop branch, the doorposts are painted. This is a liturgy of symbolism. It will not build cities to Pharaoh, but the City of God. Death will pass over those Jews who engage in the ritual. They, in turn, will pass over the border of Egypt, later they will pass over the Reed Sea, finally they will pass over the River Jordan to end their wanderings and enter the Promised Land.

With the commands to perform the first Passover, the *nomos* (law) transforms the narrative into Mythos—the formation story of a people. Now the grumbling slaves are ennobled. Their very story will be recited for generations hence. They are not only being liberated, they have become the very paradigm of redemption. The dual tracking of the Passover laws assures that they do not merely pass over physical objects, but they celebrate the Passover. Memory is invoked as necessary to celebration. In remembering, in retelling, in reenactment, the exodus of the Jews from Egypt becomes The Exodus.

As practical psychology it serves a useful purpose. The ritualization of the first paschal meal diverts the attention of the Israelites from the slaughter of the Egyptians going on around them. The diversion is mitigated, perhaps, by the despoilation of the Egyptians—the Jews can hardly ignore what is happening when they go to loot their neighbors of silver and gold. But this, too, betrays a certain wisdom. Freedom from oppression often has its first steps in looting, even bloodshed. It is the brilliance of Exodus to move beyond the riotous behavior and to regulate it to a higher cause. The Passover meal brings the Israelites back to home and hearth, surrounded by family.

As a moment of religious psychology, it proves Rashi right. He understands that Exodus 12 *is* the very essence of the Torah, a fitting place for true Instruction (for that is the meaning of Torah) to begin. All of the story now has a point: the rituals by which the people Israel remember their debt to God for their liberation from bondage. It is, in itself, a liberating ritual, for though they are bound by the rigors of its detail, they are freed by the meaning of the performance. It is one thing to eat a roast lamb with the family, it is another thing entirely to eat it as the Paschal Lamb, over which the memory of freedom is ritually invoked.

The events of the first Passover become metahistorical. Even as they are happening there is a consciousness that these events will be remembered, referred to in the future as a starting point for something new. Surrounded by the anguished cries of the Egyptians, cries that harmonize all too well with the experiences of the Israelites in Egypt, those same Israelites find a complex of responses. They respond as humans, sharing the anguish of Egyptians who, now, also have lost children to the madness of Pharaoh. Yet they have a sense of retribution as they see their oppressors get theirs. They feel the exaltation of slaves now in possession of their master's riches. Perhaps they even feel some remorse for their triumphalism.

Beyond the moment, however, the slaves fear the future. Will they, in fact, escape? And if so, what then? Assuming Moses can free them, can he lead them? Will they survive? Do they have the where-withal to transform from slaves to a free society? And who is this God to whom they now owe their freedom and their lives? What will God demand? Will God be a better bargain than Pharaoh? It is important to remember that in Hebrew the verb for service of God is the same verb as for slavery to Pharaoh, *'avodah*. The Israelites must wonder what forms their next service will take.

If they had the foresight, they might debate the benefits of a tribal confederation versus those of a unified people in covenant under God. Perhaps a Publius would arise to offer Federalist Papers to argue out the pros and cons of the nation they might become. They could spend their forty years in the wilderness as though in Philadelphia, forging a constitution and attendant amendments. But these are the original Israelites, fleeing not from George III but from Pharaoh. There will be no representative democracy, at least not yet. Three thousand years or so must pass to get to Madison, Hamilton, and Jay. On the timeline to our current form of govern-ment, it is still midnight.

But the Israelites are hardly yearning for Publius, Washington, or Jefferson. They have their Moses and, willy-nilly, their God. The civilization that was Egypt, the very civilization which they built and which enslaved them, is in ruin, rubble around their feet. The Israelites still have a long road of their own to tread. They must leave Egypt immediately. All else can follow, but only afterward. For now, the time has come to go.

DEBTS

And so the Egyptians pressed the people hard, hurrying them to leave the land, for the Egyptians said, "We all are dying!"

So the people took up their dough before it had leavened, their kneading bowls being bound up in their garments, upon their shoulders. The Israelites asked the Egyptians for vessels of silver and gold, and garments, as Moses had instructed. And the Egyptians gave them, for God had made the people graceful in their eyes. Thus they despoiled the Egyptians.

The Israelites journeyed from Ramses toward Succoth, approximately 600,000 marching men, not counting minors. A ragtag rabble of others went out with them, too, as well as sheep and cattle, a heavy number of livestock. They then baked the dough they had brought out of Egypt into rounds of flat-bread that was unleavened, for they were driven out of Egypt and could not tarry. They did not make provisions. The Israelites had dwelt in Egypt 430 years, and at the end of that 430 years, in the heart of that very day, all of the hosts of God left the land of Egypt.

It was a watch-night for God to take them out of Egypt. This night of God would be watched by all Israelites for generations. God told Moses and Aaron, "This is the rule of Passover . . . all the tribes of Israel shall do it." And so, all the Israelites did as God had commanded Moses and Aaron. . . .

Then God told Moses, "Set aside every firstborn for me. Every first-one-from-the-womb of the Israelites, whether human or beast belongs to Me."

Moses told the people, "Remember this day when you left Egypt, away from slavery; for by strength of hand God took you from this—do not eat leaven . . . and when God brings you to the land of the Canaanite, the Hittite, the Amorite, the Hivvite, and the Jebusite which God has sworn to your ancestors to give to you, to give you a land flowing with milk and honey, then you shall do this service in this month. . . . You shall tell your child on that day, 'This is because of what God did for me when God took me out of Egypt.' This shall be a symbol on your hand, and a memorial above your eyes—so that God's teaching be in your mouth—because God took you out of Egypt with a strong hand. Observe this rule in its season, day by day. . . .

"Transfer every first-one-from-the-womb to God . . . and when on the morrow your child asks you, 'What does this mean?' you can answer, 'God took us out of Egypt with a strong hand. For when Pharaoh hardened to the idea of sending us out, then God killed every firstborn in the land of Egypt, every human firstborn and every animal's firstborn. That is why I sacrifice every male first-one-from-the-womb and every firstborn of my own children I redeem.'" (Exod. 12:33–13:15)

When the momentous event that all are waiting for finally happens, everything jumbles together at once. The narrative trips over itself in its haste to get the Jews out of Egypt. The effect is somewhat like watching live coverage on CNN. The camera flits from here to there, scene upon scene is recorded and we wait, perplexed, for some analysis. What is it that we have witnessed? How significant is it? Will it be remembered? Will we be asked by our children: "Where were you when it happened?" just as we may each remember where we were when we heard that John Kennedy was shot or Richard Nixon had resigned or Princess Diana had finally crashed. The wonder of modern media is the acute awareness inside the event that it has moment. The very presence of the CNN camera bestows significance upon the event.

The Exodus from Egypt happened far too long ago to have been televised by CNN or to be illuminated by the paparazzi's flash. But within the Exodus account is that same acute awareness of its moment and significance. It would be remembered. Indeed, the departing slaves are commanded to remember, thus elevating the event beyond themselves for all generations. Still, the actual Exodus remains a jumble. It is upon us, with the gift of hindsight, to sort the moment, see the various forces pulling, the voices demanding media attention.

There are two geographical foci in this account, as there are throughout not only the book of Exodus but most of the Torah itself. The land of Egypt, even standing nuked and smoldering as it is by this point in the story, remains the central scene of action. We expect to see Christiane Amanpour with microphone in hand telling us of another battle-scarred landscape and people. But this is the original scene of battle, the first liberation that serves as the model for all others in the long religious history of the Western world. And as such, the screen includes glimpses of another land, a land of promise, a home for refugees.

The land of Israel looms on the horizon as a country already with historic associations for the Israelites. Yet even this glimpse of the Holy Land is tinted so that we see a long struggle for its conquest by the very slaves who are now being lifted from their enslavement. Even the moment of liberation recognizes that for the Israelites to come to the Promised Land, other nations yet have to be displaced. Sacred history invokes the memory of freedom, yet recognizes that others of God's creatures, be they Egyptian, Canaanite, or Jebusite, still have battles to lose and subjugation to endure. The "land flowing with milk and honey" must first flow with the blood of its inhabitants if Israel is to possess it. There is more than one side to this story. So long as there is awareness of "event," there is recognition of another point of view just beyond camera range.

Again, the narration of events is mixed together with commandments for ritualization and reenactment. Narrative and law, mythos and *nomos* remain the controlling metaphysics of the Exodus account. There is much to be said for this tendency, it changes slaves into a people who can become a covenant nation. It elevates the broken bones and aches of slavery to ennoble the Israelites as dedicated to God. It takes the despicable and downcast and makes them the chosen, the firstborn, the very "hosts of God." And it subtly turns Moses from spokesperson of God and Israel into spokesperson of God *to* Israel. In a flash, on that "watch-night" when Moses told the people to perform the Passover rituals, Moses was transformed from liberator to lawgiver.

But even as lawgiver he plays the role of commentator, telling the Israelites the significance of the event they are experiencing. He commands them, "Remember this day . . . tell your children . . . this shall be a symbol . . . so that God's teaching be in your mouth." By instructing the slaves to remember and to tell, Moses informs them of the momentousness of the occasion. This is the Passover, it shall be so for all time. You were there, he informs them. You, slaves, are coming to freedom. Your children and your grandchildren and their grandchildren for generation after generation, long after you have conquered and settled the Promised Land that was promised to our grandparents and their grandparents generations ago, they will remember *us,* we who were slaves and are now free. This event is significant, we are significant, *you* are significant. You overthrew the might of Pharaoh, you will form a new civilization to overshadow the one you built with your hands. Now, with the help of God, indeed, in covenant with God, you will build a nation, a civilization of spirit, of faith, of ritual, of law. When Moses commands the slaves to remember, he commands them to pride, self-esteem, and the beginnings of transformation from slavery to nationhood.

Again and again, these commands extend to future generations. Moses tells the slaves, "You shall tell your child on that day, 'This is because of what God did for me when God took me out of Egypt.'" The earliest rabbinic commentaries on this passage understand that this command makes all future generations feel the occasion and its significance, much as it did for the slaves themselves. The Mishnah on Passover, dating from the late second century, focuses on the phrasing of Moses' command: "In every single generation each individual must perceive himself as though he or she personally experienced the exodus from Egypt, as it is said in Scripture, 'tell your children on that day . . . what God did for me . . .'"

The significance of this command extending throughout the generations is underscored by a late medieval Yemenite commentary that points to the same "did for me" in the command. It notes, "this teaches that every individual Israelite was worthy to have those miracles performed on his or her behalf." In other words, the rabbinic tradition understands God and Moses' motivations for the commandments to remember as commands to pride, self-esteem, and transformation.

There is more than mere remembrance and recitation commanded here. Moses demands symbolic action as well. The action requires binding upon the arm and head, the seats of strength and intellect. It is not entirely clear in the Bible just what is meant to be the "symbol on your hand" or the "memorial above your eyes." But from prerabbinic times until this very day, observant Jews bind leather boxes, wound with leather straps, upon their arms and around their heads. Inside each box are passages of Scripture, including our passage here, each written upon leather parchment. The earthy physical act of binding leather is not meant to be kinky, but to be a visceral reminder, a reenactment, so that "God's teaching be in your mouth—because God took you out of Egypt with a strong hand."

This linkage of ancient ritual with the events of the Exodus plays out in a second of our passages, when the Israelites are commanded to "set aside every firstborn." This text, too, is among those bound in the leather boxes, but its complete enactment was more far-reaching in ancient times, and to a lesser extent still today. Among the livestock that the Israelites plundered from Egypt, each female gave birth to a firstborn animal. One assumes that the remnant of the flocks and herds were used for dairy products, wool, and, rarely, meat. The maintenance of the herds was a priority for the Israelites, for other than these herds, they were unable to eat on their own in the wilderness. Indeed, the biblical text makes a point of telling us that they left without provision. But of that, more later.

The firstborn of each animal was dedicated, set aside, to God. This is a polite way of saying sacrificed. The slaughter of the first-born animal to God may seem shocking to our modern sensibility, but it was a commonplace throughout the biblical world. The gods, as well as God, were propitiated by animal offerings. In this particular case, God claims the firstborn animal as properly belonging to God in repayment of debt for the redemption from Egypt. It is presented in our passage as a quid pro quo. God took Israel out of Egypt by slaying the firstborn of every Egyptian, therefore every Israelite owes the firstborn of their flocks and herds to God. The debt is eternal. From the time of the exodus onward, Israelites owe a debt to God, the sacrificial slaughter of the firstborn animals. This offering is in addition to the paschal lamb offered each year in commemoration of the Passover—for that offering provides the family meal. Firstborn animals belong to God. Israel must pay the debt it owes for redemption from Egypt.

This practice of sacrificing firstborn animals persisted throughout Jewish history up to the destruction of the Second Temple in Jerusalem by the Romans in the year 70 C.E. Since the biblical book of Deuteronomy precludes sacrifices outside of the Jerusalem Temple, there has been no sacrifice of firstborn animals for more than nineteen hundred years. I am dubious that the practice of firstborn animal sacrifice will be reinstituted at any time in the near future.

But there is a further debt to be paid to God, as Moses makes clear in this passage. Every firstborn son also belongs to God. The story of Exodus almost demands that this be so. At the outset of our story, Jewish baby boys were being drowned in the Nile River by Pharaoh. God saved them by destroying the firstborn boys of Egypt. It stands to reason, then, that Jews owe a firstborn-boy debt to God for that salvation. Like the animals, it is meant to be a perpetual debt. This apparently simplistic reasoning demands some unpacking. First, let it be clear that these boys are *not* meant to be slaughtered as sacrifice to God. Rather, they are to be dedicated to service to God. Most Bible scholars—and that includes the ancient rabbinic commentators, too—assume that this cadre of firstborn boys served as a priesthood to God. It was they, the firstborns, who would offer the sacrifices of

the firstborn animals. It would, I suppose, engender a certain grati-
tude on their behalf for their deliverance. A sort of "there but for the
grace of God go I" feeling as they slit the throat of a firstborn calf or
goat or sheep. Given the alternative, service to God must have
seemed infinitely preferable.

In time, this institution came into conflict with another group's
service to God. The descendants of Aaron became the priests who
offered sacrifice. Whatever politics may be behind the replacement
of one group for another over control of the Temple's sacrificial service (and its privileges) is not appropriate for discussion here—nor
am I qualified to offer an opinion on the politics of those vying for
the priesthood in the Israelite community following the Exodus.
What is clear from Scripture is that in a short while the transformation was complete and the firstborns no longer had any meaningful
service to render to God as priests; the Levite priests now did that
job. By then it was also clear that whatever debt the firstborn boys
still owed God, it would not be paid for with their lives. A dispensa-
tion was found whereby a firstborn Israelite male could be
redeemed of his debt to God by buying out his term of service. The
families of firstborn boys paid a fee in silver to the Levitic priests and
received a quittance from their requirement of service to God. Once
they paid their shekel they were free of their debt to God for
redemption from Egypt. Payment of the redemption price repaid
the debt to God for redemption of Israelites from slavery, which
itself was paid for with the price of the death of firstborn Egyptians.
The chain of debt was as long as the road to redemption.

Moses understands that for the people to be free, they must pay
their debts. This not only allows them to acknowledge their past
obligations to God but to depend on God for future benefits. They
need to have established a good credit record, as it were. Moses, who
grew up in the urbane surroundings of Pharaoh's household, understands this concept. But he could also have learned this lesson in
leadership economics during his years as a flock manager. Now that
his flock is Israel, the management techniques stay the same, even if
the mode of redeeming the individual members of the flock differs
somewhat.

Before we continue with our story, we should still discuss a few
aspects of plot development. We are poised to wonder, Will the

Israelites leave Egypt? Will Pharaoh allow them to be free? Will the Jews obey Moses as their leader? Indeed, will Moses succeed as a leader of humans or is he but a mere shepherd? Like the cowboy epics that I grew up with in the first decades of television, we ask these questions even as we implore you to stay tuned. But instead of breaking for a commercial, we step away from the metaphysical implications of the meaning of the story and look, instead, at the physics of the story. We still have matzo crumbs to contend with, along with other bumps in the road out of Egypt.

Let us start with matzo, that unleavened flat bread that the Jews ate then and still eat now in commemoration of the Exodus. It, too, serves the function of remembering and reenactment. But eating matzo, dreadful and burdensome as it may be to eat—go try to make a good sandwich out of two pieces of matzo—it is eaten in commemoration and not, apparently, out of debt. We eat matzo at the Passover seder and call it the bread of affliction. As a matzo manufacturer of my childhood used to advertise, "No salt. No sugar. No spices. The matzo with the taste!" Talk about your bread of affliction. At the seder, in fact, we even break the piece of matzo in half so that when we reenact the oppressive poverty of Egypt we do not even hold a full "loaf" in hand.

They ate their bread unleavened, apparently, because they did not have time for the dough to rise. The Egyptians hurried them out, they had to flee without provisions. Their kneading troughs were unavailable for the job, apparently already being packed. In haste, then, matzo got baked. It is still baked quickly. But here the biblical narrative falters somewhat. We trip, as it were, over the trail of crumbs left by the matzo. If they left so fast, what were they doing baking bread anyway? If their kneading bowls were packed, how did they make the dough in the first place? While we are asking, how did they just happen to have packed up their kneading bowls? Indeed, none of the earliest traditions translates the passage about the kneading bowls the way I have above. I follow almost all modern translations for the Hebrew of "kneading bowls," a translation that has support by use of the same Hebrew word elsewhere in the Torah with that as its clear meaning. But the very earliest translations into Aramaic, joined by many early midrash texts, say nothing about kneading bowls. For those readers of Exodus, what the Jews had wrapped up upon their shoulders was leftovers. They had eaten a Passover meal and did what any diner would do under the circumstances: They packed a doggie bag!

This seemingly whimsical interpretation helps us understand the haste with which the matzo was baked—all they had to eat as they left Egypt were some leftovers. They hastily baked matzo to accompany the meager remains. They might be able to make do with the livestock they took with them, but the lack of provision for the road bears investigation and comment. For if Moses took trouble to command them about ritual detail: matzo, bitter herbs, paschal lambs, blood on the doorposts, despoiling the Egyptians, leather bindings, and the like, you would think he might just mention that they might want to pack a hefty picnic for the road, no?

Instead, these Jews leave Egypt with herds aplenty, but nothing more to eat than a few leftovers and crumby flat bread. One can almost imagine Pharaoh coming after them by following their trail of crumbs. Either (a) these slaves gave nary a thought for the morrow—they really could not believe they could walk out of Egypt free—or (b) they had absolute faith in God that God would provide for them on whatever route God chose to bring them into the Promised Land. The fact that the subsequent biblical narrative chooses "(b) faith," when it tells us how God provided manna for the Israelites to eat for almost forty years of wandering, does not prove to me that they had any clue as to how to go about exodusing Egypt. The story line here looks as though we are meant to understand that for all the preparation, the Passover ritual, the despoiling of Egypt, and the commands Moses gave them, when the moment arrived and the gates were open, they turned and fled. They were, at that moment, for all of Moses' imprecations, still just slaves running pell-mell from their masters.

The jumble of the narrative is useful to us here as we seek to understand the events. It was chaos. Egypt had endured a nonstop bombardment of plagues. The government was in ruins. The slaves were looting the houses of their former masters. Whatever organization the leaders who opposed Pharaoh (Moses and Aaron) might have attempted to impose upon the Israelites, it was insufficient to affect the transformation of the Israelites at one fell swoop. Indeed, they would have to fight this problem out with God and Moses first for the months it took to bring them to Mount Sinai and the covenant there. Even then, they would struggle for forty years until they became organized enough as a people to conquer the land of Israel. It takes a long, long road to bring slaves to the full responsibilities of freedom.

And if we are to listen to the narrative, it is no small group of slaves who want organizing here. The awesome numbers themselves seem to preclude anything but chaos at the outset of the exodus. We read of 600,000 able-bodied men. This number *excludes* not only the children (who are mentioned), but the elderly, all females, and that group of ragtag rabble who were non-Israelites but who had "seen their opportunities and took 'em" (in the words of Plunkitt of Tammany Hall). This latter group of camp followers will be sometimes troublesome, sometimes useful—particularly when looking for a non-Israelite group on whom to pin the blame for one misdemeanor or another. But all in all, we are talking here about a group of more than two million who will be fleeing Egypt and wandering through the wilderness for the next forty years. That many fleeing slaves will not only finish off whatever economy may be left to Egypt after the plagues, it will also ensure chaos and be a formidable enemy.

There is chaos aplenty, but the numbers still defy imagining. Every modern commentary grapples with the incredible report of 600,000 plus. Some explain it to mean 600 platoons and commensurately lower the number of a platoon from thousand to hundred or some other round number. If so, that would bring the total down to just 200,000. More credible, but still difficult. I suggest that we look to the Bible's general innumeracy—particularly regarding the ages of folks in the first chapters of Genesis—and simply assume that 600,000 able-bodied men is a mite exaggerated. Let us say no more than this: A lot of Israelites left Egypt that night. The original 70 who descended with Jacob had grown manyfold. Others, non-Israelites, left with them. And when they finally left, the Egyptians, who felt themselves mortally endangered by Israel's continued presence, well, Egypt was happy to see them go.

Here, too, we look back with some jaundice at the biblical account. We have spent virtually this entire book reading how God discomfited the Egyptians who had the temerity to oppress the Jews.

We read of plagues and despoilment. But when the time comes for the Israelites to go, the Egyptians are no longer hardening their hearts and holding on to their slave force, but pushing them hard to go. So hard, in fact, that there is not even a minute for the Israelites to tarry. No time to pack provisions, only leftovers. No time, even, for dough to rise. The Jews flee Egypt in chaos, but it is not clear: Have they been led out of Egypt by the strong hand of God or have they fled Egypt during a brief window of opportunity during the chaos? As I suggested above, these are events that want interpretation. For every side of the story shown on the screen, there is another just out of camera range. The hard pressing the Jews received, the precipitous flight that precluded baking, these may be the crumbs of Egypt's point of view, a story of the Exodus that has never been shown.

CHASE

AND

AMBUSH

There was Steve McQueen driving his car in *Bullitt*. And there was Popeye Doyle skidding under the train tracks in *The French Connection*. Of course there were *Bonnie and Clyde* and then *Thelma and Louise*. It seems that every good drama must have its chase. If this were a biblical precept it would go something like "by their chase scene, so shall ye know them." There are good guys, there are bad guys, there are even bad guys who are antiheroes, and so it is not always clear who is chasing whom. Sometimes the good guys chase the bad guys. Sometimes the bad guys chase the good guys. Often in the former, the bad guys get caught. Equally, in the latter, the good guys escape. Every now and again, the scene is set so that the one being chased is hounded into a trap. But sometimes, the hare leads the hound into the trap. By the rules of dramatic permutation, this latter plot should be rare, and should come only after the conventional chase scene is very well established.

This is the real advantage of an Omniscient Narrator, a God who transcends history. For in the story of Exodus, Israel plays the role of harried hare to Egypt's bellicose hound. No sooner do the Jews leave Egypt than Pharaoh harnesses his chariot (in the movie, he would leap into a souped-up convertible, guns ablazing) and gives chase. What is unexpected to the reader, to the beleaguered Israelites, and most of all to the stunned Pharaoh and the remnant of his troops, is that the chase turns out to be an ambush. God Who Knows the plot of every Hollywood movie ever made and yet to be leads the Egyptians to their ignominious final demise. As Israel crosses the Reed Sea, which has miraculously split to reveal a road of dry land for the Jews to cross, Pharaoh follows with his troops. As Rabbi Yohanan said it in the early third century, "The minute the last Israelite ascended from the seabed, the last Egyptian descended there to give chase." The trap springs shut as the walls of water roar back to their natural state to utterly engulf the Egyptian army. They drown and the Israelites watch from the shore, safe on dry land. The script of Exodus seems to cry out for an IMAX screen.

Before we get carried away and have the credits start rolling as we fade to black, we should take a step back and view this plot twist as the social, religious, and political drama it originally was meant to be. God triumphs over the blasphemous Pharaoh. Israelite slaves find their freedom. Moses emerges as the leader to bring them into the covenant with God and to the Promised Land. A great deal of transformation must take place as this action-packed plot speeds through its climax.

> When Pharaoh sent the people out, God did not take them by the way of the Philistine's land, which was close, for the Lord said, "If the people see war, they will have regrets and then return to Egypt." So the Lord turned them toward the way to the Sea of Reeds, via the wilderness. The Israelites went up from Egypt armed.

> Now Moses took Joseph's bones with him, for he had adjured the
> Israelites saying, "When the Lord remembers you, take my bones
> with you from this place. . . ." (Exod. 13:17–19)

It is good to pause and take stock of the scene right here, just
before God baits the chase-trap for Pharaoh and his shock troops.
We know that we are coming to the climax of the story thanks to the
appearance of Joseph. The narrator even takes pains to tell us that
his appearance is not a mere literary device, introduced simply to
frame the story and alert the reader to a significant moment. Rather,
we are told that long ago, Joseph made provisions for just this
moment. Joseph apparently knew that there might be a long haul
for the Jews in Egypt. Seemingly, he even knew there would be a
Pharaoh "who knew not Joseph," who would enslave the Jews.
Surely he knew that if such were the case, God would not allow his
descendants to languish there in slavery, any more than God would
preclude him, Joseph, from having a proper burial with his ancestors in the Promised Land. And so, the text tells us, Joseph had made
his contemporaries take a vow that when God did remember to
redeem the Jews, his bones, too, should be redeemed and carried
with them back to the home country.

If all of Joseph's prophesying seems more a narrative convenience
of Exodus than an uncanny prediction of the fate of the Jews for the
centuries to follow after Joseph's death, we must turn back to the
very end of Genesis, to just before Joseph dies. You will recall that
the outset of Exodus already recalled the story of Joseph found there
when it first invoked his memory. The opening verses of the book of
Exodus drew a thumbnail sketch of the major themes of the latter
part of Genesis. Now, as the major portion of the Exodus story itself
comes to fruition, it again invokes Genesis and the story of Joseph.
As told in the last three verses of Genesis,

> Joseph said to his brothers, "I am dying. But God will remember
> you and will bring you up out of this land to the land which was
> sworn to Abraham, to Isaac, and to Jacob." Then Joseph adjured the
> sons of Israel saying, "When God remembers you, then take my
> bones up with you from this land." So Joseph died at 110 years of

age, and they embalmed him and placed him in a coffin in Egypt.
(Gen. 50:24–26)

What we see is the faithfulness of the Exodus author to his tradition. He ties up the Exodus story with an almost verbatim quote
from the end of Genesis. And although the styles of Genesis and
Exodus starkly differ, although Genesis revels in family dysfunction
and Exodus focuses on community building, for all of that, this
moment of climax firmly joins the two works together. In doing
so, it reminds us that one of the major motifs of Genesis and the
Abraham-Isaac-Jacob-Joseph story is the promise to them that they
would inherit the land of Israel. Now that the Jews have been freed
from slavery, now that Pharaoh has sent them forth, Joseph's bones
remind us of those promises of Genesis and turn our attention away
from Egypt and back to the Promised Land.

Joseph's bones also serve to set Moses off against the foil of Israel
despoiling Egypt. As the earliest rabbinic commentaries on this passage point out, all the Israelites were busy looting while pious Moses,
remembering the obligations his ancestors undertook, was busy
preparing Joseph's bones for their journey home. Moses, by this act,
links the Jewish past with the Jewish future. He remembers his forebears at the very moment that God remembers Moses' contemporaries. Israel is focused on the existential now. Moses is looking back
and yet also looking forward to a distant future, the conquest of the
Promised Land, the end of this journey. Great is the leader who can
see the end even as the journey is beginning. Greater still is the
leader who can look back and see how far he has already come along
the road.

Joseph's bones also allow Moses a moment to reflect on his own
mortality. We should remember that Moses is no youngster as the
Jews leave Egypt. At the outset of his confrontation with Pharaoh he
was eighty. We do not know how much time has passed during the
time of the plagues, but like Daniel Defoe, the ancient rabbis reckon
a "plague year." This act of kindness to Joseph's corpse presages
Moses' death—a moment we glimpsed at the outset of this book.
For the rabbis, the action Moses takes here bears fruit from God
in the end. In their own words, "as a reward for that great man
humbling himself to care for Joseph's corpse, so when Moses' time

came to die, none less than the Blessed Holy One prepared Moses for burial."

But there are yet two score years and three biblical books to get through before Moses reaches his moment upon Mount Nebo. Meanwhile, back to the chase:

> God proceeded them by day in a pillar of cloud to guide their way and in a pillar of fire by night to give them light so that they could travel day and night. The pillar of cloud did not depart from the people during the day, nor the pillar of fire by night.
>
> God commanded Moses, "Tell the Israelites to turn and camp at . . . the sea; so Pharaoh may say of the Israelites that they are confused in their geography, the wilderness has closed to them. For I have hardened Pharaoh's heart so that he will chase after you. I will gain honor through Pharaoh and his armies. Then will Egypt know that I am God!"
>
> They did so. When it was said to the king of Egypt that the people had fled, he and his servants had a change of heart. They said, "What have we done in releasing the Israelites from our enslavement of them?"
>
> So Pharaoh harnessed his chariot and took his people with him. He took six hundred prime chariots, that is to say all the chariot force of Egypt, each with its officers. God hardened the heart of Pharaoh, king of Egypt, so that he chased after the Israelites. The Israelites went forth brazenly, so that the Egyptians chased after them. Every horse-drawn chariot of Pharaoh, its drivers and troops caught up with them encamped at the sea. . . . As Pharaoh drew near, the Israelites looked up and saw the Egyptians coming after them. The Israelites were very frightened and cried out to God.
>
> Then they said to Moses, "Weren't there enough graves in Egypt that you had to take us to die here in the wilderness? What have you done to us, taking us out of Egypt? Isn't this exactly what we said to you in Egypt when we told you to leave us alone, that we would rather serve Egypt than die in the wilderness!?"
>
> Moses said to the people, "Do not fear. Stand fast and see the salvation that God will bring you today. After you see the Egyptians today you will never see them again, ever. God will do battle for you, so be silent!" (Exod. 13:21–14:14)

With terrified Israel serving as the unwilling bait, the trap is set. It is clear that God and Moses are eager to see the ultimate defeat of Egypt. They are confident that the destruction of Egypt will lead to the Israelites' confidence in their own freedom. Yet there is an almost cruel quality to the pas de deux being danced here between Moses and Israel, with God above choreographing every move. There is a quality of embrace followed by rejection. At first, God had declined to take the Israelites out of Egypt by way of the Philistine encampments, lest there be war and Israel lose heart. And yet, by the alternate route by which God leads them, Israel finds itself trapped between the pursuing Egyptians and the oncoming sea. Thus far, they have no way of knowing that they are, in fact, the bait in a trap. And so, they recoil.

In the earliest rabbinic commentary on the passage, the rabbis manage to find praise for the Israelites even in this moment of weakness. As Moses leads them back to bait the trap, it points out, the Israelites obey. They do not protest or demur for all their lack of faith. The men who realize they are heading into direct confrontation with Egypt stay mum, lest their own voiced doubts and apprehensions utterly dishearten their wives and children. Despite this bravery in the face of the advancing Egyptian army, in their hearts the Israelites fear. Why has God subjected them to such fear? Because they should have some small confidence at least that God will protect them. They have seen ten awesome plagues unleashed on their behalf. The taunting of Israel, along with Egypt, serves to remind the Israelites that they must learn faith in God.

The embrace that is counterpoint to the recoil in this dance is provided by the fire and cloud that God provides to lead them through the wilderness. God is careful that this set of symbols of God's presence serves as a constant confidence-building measure for the Israelites. Thus when Israel is sent to entrap Pharaoh, it is Moses who commands them to do so and not the pillars of cloud and fire that lead them there. Rather, these manifestations of God in nature, these miraculous signs of Presence, are taken as signs of God's enduring protection and love of Israel. As the rabbis of the Talmud understood the pillar of fire and the pillar of cloud, their presence overlapped. As the pillar of cloud began to evaporate at the end of the day, the pillar of fire arose to take its place. And as the pillar of fire extinguished each morning, the pillar of cloud sprang up to take its place. Never was there a moment that Israel lacked the reassuring presence of the pillar that represented God's existence among them. As a late medieval Yemenite commentary quotes an otherwise lost second-century source, "Even when Israel angered God, even when they rejected and insulted God, 'the pillar of cloud did not depart from the people.'"

This constancy allowed Israel to grow, to find its own way, to act out—much as would an adolescent against parents—until the Israelites matured enough as a people to come into formal covenant as partners with God. The lessons of leadership here are manifest. There is rebuke for lack of faith. There are occasions when God and Moses leave Israel to feed on their own fright—for lack of faith. But there is a concomitant commitment to a visible sign of protection. As we will see, this careful choreography will give rise, in but one more chapter, to a song and dance that are remembered and celebrated to this very day.

If Israel has its moment of regret at leaving Egypt, foolish though it may be, the Egyptians have good cause to regret having allowed their slaves to escape their service. The Egyptian economy has been ruined by the plagues and now, without the slaves, it will seem impossible to rebuild. Formerly, the Egyptians had taken Israel for granted. They were slaves. In social terms, neither they nor their troubles existed. Thus when their presence became too great a nuisance to Egypt on account of the plagues, it was deemed prudent to release them and be rid of them. There was no real recognition of their reality even then. Merely the brushing away of an annoyance. Rabbi Jonathan ben Elazar likened this to a person with a pile of cedar chips. Since they seemed insignificant, he sold them cheaply. But the buyer carefully and artfully arranged them into cedar closets and even parquet floors and walls. Only when the original seller saw them so deployed did he regret his loss.

So it was that Pharaoh and Egypt let the Jews go as slaves. But when they saw them leave Egypt, only then did they regret the loss. The trap thus set, Pharaoh harnesses his chariot force and sallies forth. As the medieval mystical work the Zohar points out, Pharaoh's 600 select chariots correspond to the 600,000 (or 600 cohorts) of Israel. This numerical allusion should tip the reader, if not the Egyptians, that God's hand is yet at work here. Israel will be protected once again. Egypt will be defeated once again. With the same blindness that has accompanied advancing armies led by demagogues for millennia, Egypt rides proudly toward its final destruction. All that Egypt can see is frightened Israel cornered between their chariots and the sea. They have not yet learned that the force which freed the oppressed would continue to assure their deliverance.

For their part, all the Israelites see is the sea before them and wave upon wave of Egyptians behind them. They, too, have yet to learn that the force that freed them from oppression would continue to assure their deliverance. They express their fears by acting out against Moses, the visible messenger of God. With biting sarcasm they spit forth their expectations that their flesh will be eaten by the desert sands. Egypt, Land of the Dead, holds more promise for them at this moment. Their cynicism will be punished. As Rabbi Israel ibn al-Naqawa wrote in mid-fourteenth-century Toledo, "One should never give an entrée to Satan. This generation of the wilderness asked sarcastically, 'Weren't there enough graves in Egypt that you had to take us to die here in the wilderness?' Thus it came to pass, for regarding them it says, 'In this very wilderness they shall meet their end, there shall they die' (Num. 14:35)."

Even for Moses it is too much. He has wrought miracle after miracle only to hear them bitch and moan. Though he begins in exhortation, telling them "stand fast," in the end he lets his guard down and just commands them to shut up. Perhaps he recognizes at this juncture that all they can do, paralyzed as they are by slave mentality and fear, is whine. But Moses is not required to listen to it. He tells them what they need to know, "God will do battle for you," since it is clear to him that they will not do battle for themselves. And since the latter is acutely obvious, he barks out the only thing that might be expected of the terrified Israelites, "Be silent!"

Despite his exasperation, Moses has not given up on his Jews. He may not have been a slave himself, but he understands them. Perhaps it is precisely because he has not tasted the lash of the overseer that Moses stands fast here. He does not fear the retribution of the overlord. Rather, he puts his faith in the Lord. He shows his sympathy for the fear-struck Israelites as he turns to God in prayer on their behalf.

But God said to Moses, "Why are you shouting at Me? Tell the Israelites to get moving! And as for you, lift up your staff and stretch your arm out over the sea and split it so that the Israelites can go through the midst of the sea on dry land. As for Me, I will harden the heart of the Egyptians so that they come after you. Then I shall gain glory through Pharaoh and all his army, through his chariots and his riders. Then will Egypt realize that I am God, when I gain glory through Pharaoh, his horses and riders."

Then the angel of God that had been preceding Israel moved behind them, so that the pillar of cloud moved from in front of them to behind them. It came between the encampment of Egypt and the encampment of Israel. Thus there were the cloud and the darkness. It illuminated the night so that the one could not approach the other all night long.

Meanwhile, Moses stretched his hand out over the sea. God moved the sea with a strong easterly wind that blew all night, making the seabed dry, so that the waters split. The Israelites went into the sea upon dry land—the water was a wall for them, to their right and to their left!

Egypt chased after them, every one of Pharaoh's steeds, his chariots, and his riders went into the sea. At the first watch of the dawn God gazed upon the encampment of Egypt in a pillar of fire and cloud, and disconcerted the Egyptian encampment. The wheels of the Egyptian chariots locked so that they drove with difficulty. Then the Egyptians said, "Let us flee from Israel, for God fights against Egypt on their behalf!"

Then God said to Moses, "Stretch your hand out over the sea so that the water returns upon Egypt, chariots and riders." So Moses stretched his hand out upon the sea and the waters returned to their full strength. At daybreak the Egyptians were fleeing directly toward it. Thus God sank the Egyptians in the sea. The waters returned and covered the chariots and the riders, all of Pharaoh's army who had followed them into the sea. Not even one of them survived.

But the Israelites walked on dry land in the midst of the sea. The water was a wall for them, to their right and to their left. So on that day God saved the Israelites from the hand of Egypt, the Israelites saw the Egyptians dead on the shore of the sea. The Israelites saw the great power that God wrought upon Egypt. Then the people feared God and believed in God and in Moses, God's servant. (Exod. 14:15–31)

Wow! Now there's a story worth retelling, a movie we could urge everyone to see again and again. The chase is fierce. The Israelites appear to be totally trapped. There seems to be bickering among the principals ("You, be silent," "Why are you shouting at Me?"). Moses changes the order of nature at God's command (or does he?). The Jews cross on dry land—easy as pie. The Egyptians walk right into the trap and get *schmeissed, zap! bam!* Viewers are left with a satisfying tracking shot of Egyptian corpses strewn on the shore, sharing the same POV as the Israelites. Cut. Print. It's a wrap. My people will call your people. We'll do lunch.

For all of the Hollywood overtones of this excellent adventure, there is theology, history, tradition, and some morals to the story still to be extracted. Let's start with the testy moment when God snaps at Moses, following Moses' having snapped at the Israelites. In the late first century, Rabbi Eliezer explained God's impatience with Moses as a practical matter. "It is as though," he suggests, "God had said to Moses, 'Moses, My children are in danger, the sea has them cut off and their enemy is pursuing them. Now is not the time for lengthy prayer.' Or it is as though God had said, 'There is a time for lengthy prayers, but now just make it snappy!'" Anyone who has sat through a modern synagogue service, particularly on the High Holidays, can appreciate Rabbi Eliezer's sentiments on behalf of God. Perhaps it is a lesson to be learned for our day and age.

The point is well taken outside of a prayer context. There are times when protracted negotiations get one a desired result. But there are also situations where it is wisest to recognize the need for urgency. At those moments it behooves all parties involved to cut to the chase and make the point as succinctly as possible.

There is yet another take on this scene, this time from a fifth-century commentary on Leviticus that takes note of our passage. In it Rabbi Elazar is quoted pointing out that at the sea Moses had all but relinquished his leadership role. There were the pillar of cloud and the pillar of fire leading Israel. This manifestation of God's leadership had allowed Moses to step to the side. But God insisted on Moses' involvement and leadership. He could not eschew his responsibilities. God tells him he must be involved, "as for you, lift up your staff and stretch your arm out over the sea." As Rabbi Elazar puts it, it is as though God tells Moses, "If you do not split the sea, no one else will do it, either." This is an important insight into God's chiding of Moses. There are seminal moments where it is essential to step up to the plate, bat in hand. Yes, Moses had already done enormous labor in getting the Israelites organized to leave and in his negotiating with Pharaoh to release them. But without this particular gesture, all of Moses' leadership would have been for naught. Israel would be lost. God reminds Moses not only that God will support him, but that he, Moses himself, must now take up the staff and split the sea. If not him, then who?

God offers support for Moses' gesture. The cloud interposes between the Israelites and the approaching Egyptians. The chase is suspended, either because the Egyptians can no longer see the Israelites for the cloud, or because the cloud physically precludes their drawing near. God does intervene in nature, it seems, as the cloud's miraculous nature is described. There is light emanating from the cloud even as it brings darkness upon all that it overshadows. In a commentary to Psalms, Rabbi Hoshaiah notes that the cloud was Janus-like at this moment. One face turned toward Egypt with darkness. Yet the second face turned opposite toward Israel and illuminated them. The warm glow of God's light brought protection, security, and succor.

But more so, we read that God gazes down upon the camp of the Egyptians striking fear and consternation. The wheels of their chariots lock, perhaps because the cloud brings rains that mire them in the mud. Perhaps, though, it is the pure miracle of God's presence. This push and pull between natural phenomena on the one hand and miracle on the other continues in the chapter through the crossing of the sea. A bit later in this book we will take a time-out to consider the nature of biblical miracles and how we are to read them. Perhaps it is possible to understand miracles in a way that satisfies our scientific worldview while still making God's grace available, even today.

I write this because our text is careful to describe the crossing of the sea in miraculous terms, but at the same time takes pains to tell us that a strong east wind blew all night to throw back the waters and dry out the path that Israel took. This sounds like a naturalist explanation with a layer of miracle superimposed. For now, we will not worry the miracle question, but instead turn to the Israelites faced with the phenomenon. These are the same Israelites whom Moses has just rebuked and told to shut up. It is they who must descend onto the seabed with the hopes that the walls of water on either side of them stay exactly where they are. In other words, miracle or none, crossing the sea demands an act of faith.

One twelfth-century commentary on this dilemma suggests that the sea did not split until the Israelites had fully demonstrated that faith. "They had to enter the water until it came up to their nostrils before the sea split for them." Two second-century sages staked out positions on the issue as follows: Rabbi Meir said that when the tribes stood assembled at the shore of the sea, each tribe vied for the privilege of descending into the waters first, so that their tribe might have the merit of causing the sea to split. But Rabbi Yehuda was less sanguine. He suggested that the tribes indeed did argue at the shore of the sea. But what they said was, "Oh, you go first, no you go first." No tribe wanted to be the first one in until Nachshon son of Aminadav finally put an end to the cowardice by jumping in and causing the sea to split for everyone.

Once again, the ancient commentaries anticipate the modern lessons. Volunteerism often works just the way the rabbis have described. In some cases you can't be first fast enough. Yet in other cases, particularly those that require a modicum of faith and carry some risk of loss, no one will lead the way—everybody takes a giant step backwards. To this very day, Nachshon ben Aminadav's name is a watchword in the Jewish community for the showing of faith and the willingness to volunteer. The reward for such exceptional bravery is redemption for the entire people.

SONG

"*Free at last, free ut last;*
Thank God Almighty,
We are free at last."
—Old Negro spiritual

I   t was an occasion that called for song. It called for song
and poetry, music and dance. The Israelites, arrayed on
the shore of the sea, could look back and see their enemy
vanquished. Truly God was great and Moses was his
prophet. And because it was a sweet moment of victory
and vindication, a moment in which the people believed
in him, Moses sang. He, who had been born a slave and was
saved by God from drowning at the hand of Pharaoh and
Egypt, now saw God requite his enemies measure for measure.
They were drowned by the sea at the hand of God. Moses, who
had been raised in the court of Pharaoh only to see another
Pharaoh become his bitter antagonist, now saw him destroyed.

Not only was Moses triumphant. God was triumphant. God had overthrown the oppressor. God reigned exalted over the haughty of Egypt and the downtrodden of Israel. It was an occasion that called for song.

It was then that Moses and the Israelites sang this song to God. Which they recited by saying.

I will sing unto God Who has truly triumphed,
Horse and rider has He thrown into the sea.
God is my strength and my song, He is my salvation.
This is my Lord whom I will praise, the Lord of my ancestor Whom I
*   exalt.*
God is a man-of-war, His name is God,
He has hurled the chariots of Pharaoh and his army into the sea,
His select officers are sunk in the Sea of Reeds.
The depths cover them, they have descended to the deep like a rock.
Your right hand, O God, is mighty in strength,
Your right hand, O God, smashes the foe . . .
The enemy announced, I'll advance against them, I'll overtake them,
I'll allot the spoils, my soul will be sated,
I'll bare my sword, my hand will enslave them.
But You breathed a breath and the sea covered them,
They sank like lead in the mighty waters.
Who among the gods is like You, God?
Who is like You—mighty in holiness, awesomely praiseworthy, doing
*   wonders?*
You stretched forth Your right hand and the earth swallowed them up.
In Your grace You led the people whom You redeemed,
In Your power You guided them to the sacred plain.
The nations heard and trembled,
Terror grabbed the Philistine settlers . . .
The officers of Edom . . . the chiefs of Moab . . .
All the settlers of Canaan melted away.
Dread and fear have befallen them . . .
Until Your people passes, O God,
Until the people whom You have conceived passes.
You will bring them and plant them on the mountain of Your possession

. . . And God shall reign for ever and ever!

For Pharaoh's horse came into the sea with his chariots and riders,
Then God turned the waters of the sea upon them,
While the Israelites walked on dry land in the midst of the sea.

Then the prophet Miriam, sister of Aaron, took a tambourine in her hand and all the women followed her, dancing with tambourines. Miriam led them in singing:

Sing unto God Who has truly triumphed,
Horse and rider He has thrown into the sea.
(Exod. 15:1–21)

Once again Miriam stands at the water's edge. This time, she has seen her prophecy fulfilled. Long ago she had predicted that she would have another brother who would save the Jews. The baby was born, placed in a basket, and set afloat while Miriam "stood watch from afar that she might know what would be done with him." In the first instance in Exodus, she was only identified as the boy's sister, she was otherwise anonymous. Here, she takes her rightful place as named matriarch of Israel, a prophet, sister of Aaron. In the Talmud, Rabbi Nahman asks why is she so identified, after all; at this moment would we not expect her to be called "sister of Moses"? But, he points out, when she took up the mantle of prophecy, it was to predict Moses' very birth, which is to say that when she was first "Miriam the prophet," she was then only the "sister of Aaron." Her merit, though profound, is tied to her brothers. Such, at first blush, was the fate of the women of Israel in those days.

Later, in the days of Deborah the prophet, women had a bit more independence. It is true that in the Book of Judges (4:4) she herself is identified as "Deborah, the prophet, wife of Lappidot." But when her turn came to sing a song, she went first, before the men sang. While Miriam did lead the women of Israel in song, it was only after the men sang. A twelfth-century commentary on this passage suggests that this was not bias against women so much as giving the right to sing first to those who had assured the victory. In the case of the Exodus, Moses and Aaron pled the case before Pharaoh, so the men sang first. In the case of Deborah, she was the general, so she led the chorus. In the fight for liberation, it seems women get liberated only if they literally fight.

In fact, the very earliest commentary on our Exodus passage gives the prophet Miriam and the Israelite women their due, "Exactly what Moses sang with the men, so sang Miriam with the women. As the Text says, 'Sing unto God Who has truly triumphed, Horse and rider He has thrown into the sea.'" The verse is the same for men and women. Liberation from slavery meant liberation for everyone. The men's chorus and the women's chorus both had their moment on stage to sing their praises to God who freed them. The Song would be repeated by every oppressed people who looked to the Lord for succor, to all who give thanks for their freedom. When the Song says, "God is my strength and my song, He is my salvation," the rabbis hear that God was, God is, and God will always be my salvation. Now and forever, hallelujah!

The poetic language of this Song is meant to be instructive to us. The earliest rabbinic commentary cites the verse "This is my Lord whom I will praise," with some bit of puzzlement. How can we praise the Lord who created heaven and earth? Are we not doomed to fail and thus diminish rather than praise God? What words or songs could we offer if "God is my strength and my song"? A clever rabbi named Abba Saul suggests that *imitatio dei* is the sincerest form of praise. How shall we praise God? Just as God is merciful and compassionate, so must we be merciful and compassionate. This is a stirring lesson of humanitarian charity to learn from the Creator. It is in the power of song that we can hear the universal message of the music.

If music is a language spoken by every human, the ancients also imagined that music echoed through the celestial spheres. Indeed, a late medieval midrash suggests that the angels themselves sang a verse just at the end of the Song. I am not clear whether this commentary is suggesting that the angels sang it instead of Israel or that they, in the heavens, sang along with Israel. It is the verse of God's enthronement. Finally triumphant over the rank pretender Pharaoh, exalted by Israel, God is proclaimed as king. The Israelites (and perhaps the angels) sing, "And God shall reign for ever and ever!" Anyone who has ever heard a public singing of this verse as it is found in its Christian version in Handel's *Messiah* will have no doubt that the message is meant to stir the hearts of humanity to love of one another. And anyone who has sung along surely knows that at the moment of joining in the chorus the truth of those words is manifest, "And He shall reign for ever and ever! Hallelujah!"

For all that the chorus sings with joy, there are certain minor notes sounded on the organ of ancient midrash. As early as the second century, following the destruction of the Jerusalem sanctuary in the year 70 C.E. by Roman legions, the rabbis turn to the verse "Who among the gods is like You, God?" Of course, they are somewhat troubled by the theology of the passage to begin with. As monotheists, they squirmed in their seats when reading a verse that seemed to admit of the possibility of "gods," even if "God" triumphs over them. The trouble they had reading about these gods—even if the verse only referred to Pharaoh and the false gods of Egypt—is that the Hebrew term was defectively written, as though to underscore the perplexity that the word inspired. Since the term in its original seemed to lack certain letters, it could be read aloud as though the word for "gods" was the Hebrew word for "the deaf." The verse would then be even odder than it appears already: "Who among the deaf is like you, God?"

The tenor of this comment is similar to theology often heard since the Nazi Holocaust. How can God sit up in heaven deaf to the cries of Israel? How can God be so restrained as to not interfere when the people Israel are enslaved and degraded, whether by Nazis or by Pharaoh and the Egyptian taskmasters? The force of the question is brutal. Why, asks the midrashist, do we have to sing a song for salvation in the first place? Where were You, God, when the Jews were being enslaved? Why did You not intervene then? What took You so long, God? The question is shocking, even bordering on blasphemous, especially in the context of the Song of the Sea. But in the post-Destruction environment of the early second century, or, for that matter, at almost any subsequent point of Jewish history, the question had a certain urgency. We would rather not have been enslaved at all than sing our chorus of thanks now, this midrash seems to say.

But it is, as I have said, a minor chord in an otherwise loud chorus of praise. The general tenor of the Song of the Sea may be characterized by one of the earliest commentaries on the verse:

"'You stretched forth Your right hand and the earth swallowed them up.' This teaches that all living souls are in the palm of the One-Who-Spoke-And-Brought-The-World-Into-Being. As it is written, 'Every living soul is in his hands' (Job 12:10) and it says, 'Into His hands I consign my spirit' (Psalm 31:6)."

Juxtaposing these verses of Job and Psalms with the Song of the Sea recalls a hot afternoon in late summer 1963, in Washington, D.C. On that day, Marian Anderson got up to sing with hundreds of thousands of blacks and whites who had marched there to help assure freedom for the African Americans in this country. Like the Israelites at the Sea they sang, "He's got the whole world in his hands."

Moses, some three thousand years earlier, heard the words of the Song not only as thanksgiving for deliverance from Egypt but as a charge for the future. Like any great leader, he understood that there was yet a long road ahead. The Song at the Sea's mention of the nations yet to be conquered filled him with dread, but also with hopes and dreams. Even as his dream of freeing the Jews from Egyptian slavery was realized, he turned his sights to the next challenge, the next dream. There is no finer midrash on Moses' state of mind and commitment to continued leadership of Israel than the one that the Reverend Martin Luther King preached on that same afternoon of August 28 in Washington. One can almost hear the words in Moses' own stuttering mouth, with but four changes of name and locale:

> I say to you today, my friends, so even though we face the difficulties of today and tomorrow, I still have a dream. It is a dream deeply rooted in the [Israelite] dream. I have a dream that one day this nation will rise up and live out the true meaning of its creed—we hold these truths to be self-evident, that all men are created equal.
>
> I have a dream that one day on the red hills of [Canaan], the sons of former slaves and the sons of former slave-owners will be able to sit down together at the table of brotherhood.
>
> I have a dream that one day, even the land of [Moab], a land sweltering with the heat of injustice, sweltering in the heat of oppression, will be transformed into an oasis of freedom and justice. . . .

I have a dream that one day every valley shall be exalted, every hill and mountain shall be made low, the rough places will be made plain and the crooked places will be made straight and the glory of the Lord shall be revealed and all flesh shall see it together.

This is our hope. This is the faith that I go back to the [Sinai wilderness] with. With this faith we will be able to hew out of the mountain of despair a stone of hope. With this faith we will be able to transform the jangling discords of our nation into a beautiful symphony of brotherhood. With this faith we will be able to work together, to pray together, to struggle together . . . to stand up for freedom together, knowing that one day we will be free. . . .

Let freedom ring, . . . from every mountainside . . . when we allow freedom to ring, when we let it ring from every village and every hamlet . . . we will be able to speed up that day when all of God's children . . . will be able to join hands and sing in the words of the old Negro spiritual,

"Free at last, free at last;
thank God Almighty,
we are free at last."

BITTER/SWEET

No sooner did the music stop than the bitching started. Following the long run of miracles they had just experienced and the happy songs they sang together, it was galling. We shall overcome, my ass. They were slaves, just slaves. They couldn't think about freedom and its responsibilities. They couldn't think about God and covenant. They couldn't think about Moses and his faithful leadership of them throughout the confrontations with Pharaoh in the palace and most recently at the shores of the sea. They were slaves, just slaves. They couldn't think, period.

Moses tried very hard not to take it personally. But it galled him to see their ingratitude to God.

Really, they were like little children. So the seawater was salty and undrinkable! Did they really expect sweet water at the salty shore? He practically had to drag them away from looting Pharaoh's charioteers washed up on the beach there. Where was their faith in the future? Now that he got them to Marah the water was still too salty to drink without a bellyache. These slaves would bellyache with or without drinking water. Whine, whine, whine. If only Moses could turn whine into water for them to drink!

> Thus Moses made the Israelites journey from the Reed Sea into the wilderness of Shur. They traveled three days without finding water. When they came to Marah they could not drink the waters, for they were bitter, which is why it is called Marah, meaning bitterness. So the people whined at Moses asking, "What can we drink?" Moses prayed to God, who instructed him regarding a piece of wood from a tree God showed him. Moses threw it into the water and the water became sweet. . . .
>
> They traveled to Elim, where there were twelve wells of water and seventy date palms. They then traveled from Elim and the entire community of Israel came to the Sinai wilderness . . . where they whined to Moses and to Aaron, "If only we had died by God's hand in the land of Egypt, where we sat by the flesh pots and ate our fill of bread. But you have taken us into this wilderness to kill the entire community by starvation!"
>
> So God said to Moses, "Now I will rain down bread from heaven so that the people may go out and glean it, day by day. Thus shall I test them, to learn whether they can follow my teachings or not. . . . For I have heard the whining of the Israelites. Tell them, 'At dusk you will eat flesh and in the morning you will be sated with bread. Thus shall you know that I am the Lord, your God.'"
>
> So it came to pass at dusk that quails ascended and covered the encampment. And in the morning there was a blanket of dew surrounding the encampment. The blanket of dew covered the wilderness, thin and flaky, thin as a frost upon the ground. The Israelites saw it and asked one another, "Man, what is this?" for they knew not what it was. But Moses told them, "This is the bread that

God has given you to eat. Here's the thing that God commanded you, each person should collect as much as he can eat. Take an omer measure per person, per tent."

The Israelites did so, they gleaned: some more, some less. When they measured the omer, the one who had taken more had no extra, nor did the one who had taken less lack any. Each had gleaned what they needed to eat. Then Moses told them, "No one may leave any over till the morning." But they did not listen to Moses and so some people did keep extra until the morning. It bred maggots and turned rancid. Moses was short-tempered with them.

They gleaned it each morning, each according to his appetite, and when the sun warmed up, it evaporated. On Friday, they would glean a double portion of bread, so that each person had two omers. The chieftains of the community came to inform Moses. He said to them, "This is what God spoke of, the Cessation, for tomorrow is the Holy Sabbath of God. If you want to bake, bake. If you want to boil it, boil—but leave a remnant preserved until morning."

They left it until morning, as Moses had commanded. It did not turn rancid nor did worms breed in it. Moses told them, "Eat of it today, for it is God's Sabbath, so today you will not find it in the fields. . . ." Yet on Saturday some of the people did go out to glean, but they could not find it. God asked Moses, "How long will you refuse to observe My commandments and my teachings? Look, God gave you the Sabbath, which is why God gave you two days' bread on Friday."

The Israelites called it manna. It was like coriander seed, but white. It tasted like honey-dipped wafers. . . . The Israelites ate manna for forty years, until they came to inhabited land. They ate manna until they came to the border of Canaan. (Exod. 15:22–16:35)

Bread and water, water and bread. Day by day, day by day. Nothing could better mark the life of a slave than bread and water, day by day. The bread tasted sweet to them, and the water, though bitter, became sweet. Day by day for forty years the children of Israel— slaves—whined their way through the wilderness.

I suppose one shouldn't blame them too harshly for their fears at Marah. No water to drink is a serious matter. Dying of thirst must be unimaginably terrifying. In the book of Genesis, when Abraham threw his Egyptian wife and her son, Ishmael, into the wilderness, the lad wept for fear of dying of thirst. Now that Egypt has returned the favor and thrown the descendants of Abraham into the wilderness, they, too, weep for the same fear.

On the other hand, they had just seen God part the waters. They had just walked through the sea on dry land. They had just seen their oppressors drown before their very eyes. They believed in God and in Moses, God's servant. But not for long. They needed their daily water miracle. It was not just water they craved, but a fix. They had become miracle addicts. Show us another miracle. Change the course of nature for us again. As Rabbi Levi archly remarked in the early fourth century, Scripture has it just exactly right, "they could not drink the waters of Marah, for they were bitter."

Rabbi Levi appreciates the subtlety of the verse, which has a pronoun in its second half. "They were bitter" refers not just to the water at Marah but to the slaves themselves. Embittered by their years of slavery, disoriented by the plagues and the suddenness of the Exodus, distrustful of Moses' authority and even more so of the new Master, God, they were bitter. They could not swallow all that was happening to them. The generation of the wilderness, as they came to be called, were connoisseurs of bitterness. As we will see, their kvetching about their liquids becomes a motif for the remainder of the generation. They will drive Moses to violence before the journey is finished.

God is, at least for the moment, more sympathetic to their complaining. God realizes that the children of Israel are but slaves, dependent on their master for their daily bread. God offers Moses a way to sweeten the waters of Marah and then has Moses lead them to an oasis of twelve wells and date palms to sweeten the deal. The dates ooze honey, a foretaste of the land they have been promised. But when once again confronted with the barren wilderness of Sinai, not yet able to scout the wells and shrubs that would slake their thirst, the Israelites turn to pitiable bathos. They wail, "If only we had died by God's hand in the land of Egypt." The earliest rabbinic comment on the passage puts these wimps in their proper context. It imagines them saying, "We should have died during the plague of darkness in Egypt!" In other words, from the very first time the rabbis read this passage they had these guys reduced to a

Jewish mother joke: How many Jewish mothers does it take to change a lightbulb? One, but she doesn't change it. Instead she says, "It's okay, I'll just sit here in the dark." How many Israelites does it take to find water in the Sinai? Six hundred thousand. But they don't drink it; they'd rather die there in the dark.

God still is sympathetic to those Israelites, even if their rabbinic descendants may joke about them. No water? No food? Have no fear. God will send bread from heaven to feed the multitude. And as an appetizer, a little hors d'oeuvre of quail. Bony, yes, but tasty roasted on a spit over an open flame. And apparently easily trapped as they fly low over the encampment of the Israelites, exhausted by their journey through the wilderness—the quail, that is, not the Israelites. They, too, will be exhausted by their journey, but as we will see in just two more chapters, under God's protection those rag-tag slaves are much less easy prey. The quail, however, are theirs for the taking.

In fact, the quail are so easily caught that perhaps the Israelites mistake whether it is a miracle at all. When, on the morrow, God sends the manna, the Jews receive it as a miracle and continue to do so six days a week for the next forty years. This is no small miracle, even if the rabbis later quibble among themselves as to when exactly the rain of manna ceased to fall. In any case, the manna was so plentiful that the Israelites soon grew bored with it. And then, in the face of "daily bread" in the very wilderness, those shameless curs asked God for quail again, instead. The story, though embarrassing, is instructive. It is told at length in the biblical book of Numbers, chapter eleven.

> . . . The Israelites, too, wept, and said, "Who will feed us meat? We remember the fish we ate in Egypt, the cucumbers and watermelon, the leeks, onions, and garlic. Now we are dried out—we see nothing, nothing but manna!"
>
> . . . Then Moses said to God . . . "Where will I get meat to give to all these people? For they cry to me, 'Give us meat that we may eat.' I cannot do it alone, it is too hard for me. . . ."
>
> So God said to Moses . . . "Tell the people to sanctify themselves tomorrow and they shall eat meat. For you have cried into God's ears saying, 'Who will feed us meat? It was better for us in Egypt.'

So God will give you meat and you shall eat. Not for one day will you eat, nor for two, not for five days, nor ten, nor twenty. A full month, until it comes out of your nostrils, until it is disgusting—because you have rejected God who was in your midst and cried to him asking, 'Why did we have to leave Egypt?'"

Moses said, "Six hundred thousand stand the people in whose midst I am and You say I shall give them meat that they will eat an entire month! Can one slaughter enough sheep and cattle to satisfy them? Can one gather enough fish from the sea to satisfy them?"

God asked Moses, "Is God's arm too short? Now you shall see if My word comes to pass or not!" . . . Then a wind rushed forth from God and swept quails from the sea. They were strewn upon the camp, covering an area of one day's journey square, two cubits off the ground. The people arose all that day and all that night and all the next day gathering quails. The very least gathered ten bushels. They were spread all over the camp.

The meat was yet between their teeth, still uncut, when God's anger flared against the people. God struck them with a very great plague. That place was called Graves-of-Lust. For there they buried those who lusted . . .

Although Graves-of-Lust sounds a bit too much like an X-rated video, the point of the biblical narrative is clear. Miracles are not to be scoffed at. Miracles should not engender boredom as a response. God's beneficence may be rejected, but there will be a price to pay. Satisfaction with the mundane miracle, if you will, is far preferable to whining. Oh, God will give you what you whine for—until it comes out of your nose. My son Alexander, an avid bird watcher, points out to me that the "quail" of this passage were unlikely, the range of quail disqualify them as the Hebrew, *slav,* of this passage. He suggests instead translating it as "sand-grouse." I rather like grouse as the rendering—along the lines of God saying to the Israelites: "You wanna grouse about the food? Fine, I'll give you so much damn grouse you'll puke!" God will pour forth so much abundance that even the most obdurate whiner will become disgusted with the endless appetite of the slave mentality. One must learn to be satisfied with the little miracles God rains down from heaven daily.

The day-in day-out nature of manna, six days a week, fifty-two weeks a year for forty years, is stultifying. It is so easy to forget the awesomeness of the daily miracle and turn against it in complaint. There is a pernicious testing here of God by Israel. They constantly push God in their collection of the manna. First, they collect more than their omer full. Immediately, the size of their portions is reduced to the omer they have been allotted. While God makes it clear, "each according to his need," God equally makes it clear that an omer per person will suffice.

Being slaves, the Israelites quite naturally wish to store some of the manna away against the morrow, when there may no longer be food to eat. Too long they endured the caprice of their Egyptian masters. They had learned the hard way that food rations must not be consumed entirely, they must be hoarded. And so they keep back a bit, against Moses' command. It is only natural for slaves to have done so. God cruelly turns the leftovers into rancid rot, crawling with worms. God does not warm to being tested by God's ungrateful creatures.

The Israelites are given another opportunity to display their faith, to show that they understand that God as Master is not at all the same as Pharaoh as Master. If God says God will provide, then they need not fear. But they are slaves and fear they do. So despite the double portion of manna that falls on Fridays, to preclude labor on the Sabbath, there are still those who go out seeking manna on Shabbat. God's wrath is provoked by those of little faith who violate God's Sabbath. As the earliest commentary on Exodus imagines it, they respond by asking Moses a question about the Sabbath provoked by the Passover experience, "Moses, our teacher," they ask, "how is this day different from all other days?" One would think that slaves would quickly warm to a day of leisure each week. Alas, old habits, especially habits long ingrained by slavery, die hard.

Israel also does not warm to being tested by God. The daily miracle of manna requires that they gather no more than one day's portion—with no provision for the morrow. They already fled Egypt with matzo, the bread of affliction that did not even rise. Now they had manna, but God would not give them more than one day's supply at a time. This makes the Israelites wholly dependent upon God for their sustenance—a condition that does not enhance their sense of security and so serves to undermine their belief. It is too much to expect of slaves who have been freed to return to such abject dependence upon their Master, even if that master be God.

Of course, this daily dependence is precisely God's point. The Israelites must learn this basic fact of belief if they are ever to enter covenant with God. Each moment of their individual existence depends upon God. Whether it is their daily bread or forgiveness of sins; in fact, every breath they draw, every moment of existence depends upon God's grace and daily miracles. Manna is a powerful teacher. It teaches to be satisfied with bread from heaven, with clear skies and sweet water. Do not lust for what you do not need, for such lust will bury you. As Rabbi Eliezer taught it, Let today's bread suffice to give you faith that you will not hunger tomorrow.

Although Rabbi Eliezer sensed the heart of the test implicit in the daily portion of manna, he refrained from remarking on its miraculous nature. It is true, a daily portion, 6 days × 52 weeks × 40 years, is a very long running miracle. But other rabbis reveled in the special nature of the manna itself. Perhaps this tendency to fantasize about the manna came from the varying descriptions of it in Exodus and in Numbers. The fact that it fell daily led one medieval authority to speculate that the manna was eaten hot, like bread from the oven, rather than cold or at "room temperature." A second-century source remarks on the ability of one omer to fill the appetite of each Israelite, "When the hero Nachshon son of Aminadav, who was the first Israelite to cross the Reed Sea, went to gather manna, he and his household would gather buckets; while the modest pauper would gather but a smidgen. Yet when they each arrived at their respective tents, lo, each had an omer of manna." In the mid-third century, Rabbi Yosi ben Hannina said, "Manna tasted differently for each person who tasted it. For young men it tasted like bread, for old folks like wafers dipped in honey, for babies like milk from a mother's breast, for the sickly like porridge. When idol worshipers tasted it, it was bitter." And, by the ninth century, manna had become "any taste a person desired; whether bread or meat or honey or milk or butter. . . ."

All this from manna, a food that led the Israelites to ask, "Man, what is this?" While the question gave manna its name—for the pun is intended—the essence of the miracle may be at the very heart of the question. By this point in our story those Israelites were literally glutted with miracles. To take a leaf from the rabbis, yet once more, if there were miracles involved in the plagues of Egypt and Israel's deliverance, there were ten times as many miracles in their survival in the wilderness. To put it another way, and so reiterate what I pointed out above, day by day God grants innumerable miracles. One need not experience the parting of the Reed Sea to recognize the tiny miracle of a hot loaf of bread. One need not see the Nile turn to blood to behold the miracle of the sun, rising in the east over the peaks in the wilderness.

When I was yet a teenager I paid a visit to the wilderness of Sinai. There, with the impeccable timing of experienced tour guides, we were awakened at four A.M. to a night of glistening stars. The mountains loomed high above us as we peeked out from our sleeping bags arrayed under the buses—this to avoid being nibbled by bedouin camels. Rousted from our warm and cozy nests, we were set to climbing Jebel Moussa, Mount Moses. This was the mountain that local Arab tribes had long ago agreed was the mountain where God first told Moses of his mission to Egypt and which he later climbed to receive the Ten Commandments. This was the mountain sanctified by the monastery of St. Catherine perched at its foot, where the monks carefully tend a rosebush they claim was the very one that burned for Moses.

We climbed through the end of night, guided by the moonlight, hiking ever upwards on unsteady legs. It was not the tallest mountain in the range, but the shivers it gave us came not from the dewy chill but from a sense of sacred place. As we reached the summit we looked west to see the moon setting over the land of Egypt. When we turned eastward the sun was breaking upward over the mountains of Midian, in Saudi Arabia. The sense of miracle was palpable, even for our group of upper-middle-class suburban American teens—no slaves we, but the descendants of slaves who beheld the same sight daily.

The problem with miracles is that they are in the eye of the beholder. God may send bread from heaven, but the scoffer sees an edible excretion of plant sap. God may split the sea, but the cynic consults the meteorologist to explain the wind, tides, and shore conditions. Slaves have a hard time holding on to the sense of the numinous necessary to appreciate or even apprehend the miracles that take place around us daily. The late Professor Abraham Joshua Heschel called this ability "radical amazement." It is a phenomenon almost anyone can feel in the presence of a newborn baby, the experience of the "miracle" of ten perfect little toes and ten more baby fingers.

Many American Jews had a cognizance of the miraculous when Israel won the Six-Day War some thirty years ago, or again when they successfully raided Entebbe to rescue their citizens less than ten years later. But the feeling of the miraculous, almost by definition, requires a time-out from the ordinary. Something must occur that seems, to the recipient of the beneficence, to overturn the laws of nature. That is precisely how God's intervention in the moment is most easily apprehended. Yet for others, the mere coincidence of the fortunate moment with the requirement of the time suffices for recognition of God's presence. For yet others, the very existence of the loaf of bread—let alone manna from heaven—is proof positive of the miracle. The late Rabbi Max Kadushin spoke of a category of rabbinic thought he called "normal mysticism." He coined this oxymoron to explain how the rabbis felt that daily events could be employed to manifest God's presence, hence the mystical. This mystical experience of God's presence is a recognition of the miraculous in our very private lives, in our families, in our community at large, even in a nation.

God and Moses seek to transform the 600,000 slaves and their families into a nation of believers. There is a moment, at the Reed Sea, when seeing the destruction of Egypt as the culmination of the Exodus, the people do believe. They believe in miracles and, through them, in God and Moses. But the manna sets them a harder task: a belief in God without the pyrotechnics of chariots, war, and crashing waters. A bowl of bread, with no thought for the morrow, becomes the vehicle of belief. No longer is the focus on the miracle that screams "time must have a halt." Instead, the manna requires that a full stomach, one day at a time, must suffice. God tests the slaves on this very point, so that whitebread alone, as it were, the very symbol of the monotonous mundane, becomes sufficient to inspire belief in God.

Without this belief, the Israelites will be stranded on the road to redemption. They will be slaves who have escaped Egypt, but no more. It is Moses' task to lead them. Not to the Promised Land, which as the crow flies is but a few days' distance, for the physical journey will take forty years. Rather, Moses must lead them to believe in the daily presence of God in their lives. It is that metaphysical belief that will enable Israel to unite, if only momentarily, and enter into covenant with God.

In the end, their physical journey weighs them down. They remain slaves who will die in the desert. Their concern for their daily welfare is too ingrained to abandon the desire for bread and water, water and bread. Day by day, day by day. Despite the water of the Nile, which turned to blood. Despite the waters of the Reed Sea, which stood to attention for them as they crossed through it on dry land. Despite the twelve springs, which flowed sweetly for them at Elim. Despite even the bitter waters of Marah, which Moses sweetened. In the end, they remained slaves whom all the waters of creation could not have washed clean of their whining disbelief.

WATER
FALL

Like all meticulously observed rituals, my late uncle Joe's Passover seder behavior was predictable and, in its own way, a reassurance. Following the meal, when everyone else in the family was redistributing the Passover Haggadahs so that we could have the necessary script for the after-meal seder rituals in hand, Uncle Joe retreated to the nearest couch. He always carried with him the blue glass soda siphon. After noisily wooshing his glass full of seltzer he would drink the entire contents in seemingly one long swallow. We children waited impatiently for the eruption to follow. A long, satisfied *greps* (Yiddish slang for a watery burp) left us tittering while the adults commented, "Feh, Joe, such a *chazzer.*" That last word was the epitome of refined judgment—for a *chazzer* was a pig, and everyone knew that a pig had no place at a kosher table.

A kosher for Passover table, no less. Every item guaranteed kosher by some rabbi or another, down to the fizzy water that Uncle Joe swilled from the blue bottle. He may have *grepsed* dyspeptically, but the idea of Kosher for Passover water makes me ready to shout at the rabbi who put his okay on the bottle, "Feh, such a *chazzer!*" Imagine the chutzpah of some rabbi telling me that water is kosher. Water, by definition, is kosher. And that a rabbi might profit from this type of scam does more than render me dyspeptic. It makes me apoplectic, because it is nothing less than theft to make a profit on the pious gullability of Jewish consumers.

I tell you of this pet peeve of mine not merely to vent my spleen—although I admit it is almost as satisfying for me to do so as Uncle Joe's eructation was for him—but to make a point about water. When the wrong words are invoked over that precious liquid, it has the potential to arouse ire. On one hand, my sense of slapstick begs me to take the soda siphon and, squeezing handle down, turn it sideways to douse all within range. But on the other hand, the juxtaposition of water with Passover leads to a discussion of the deprivation that the Israelites continually suffered in the wilderness. Their lack of fresh water was matter for ire. And the only slapstick that took place there in the Sinai was literal, not figurative.

Let's let the text of Exodus explain that last remark.

> The entire Israelite confederation traveled . . . and encamped at Rephidim, but there was no water for the people to drink. The people quarreled with Moses, saying, "Give us water to drink!"
>
> Moses said to them, "Why do you quarrel with me? Why do you test God so?"
>
> But the people thirsted for water. They whined to Moses saying, "Why, then, did you take me up from Egypt to kill me and my children and cattle with thirst?"
>
> Moses cried to God, "What shall I do with this people, soon they will stone me!"
>
> God told Moses, "Pass before the people and take some of the elders with you. Take in your hand the staff with which you struck

the Nile. Go, and I will stand with you there on the rock at Horev. Strike the rock so that water comes forth from it, that the people may drink."

Moses did so in the sight of the Israelite elders. And he called the name of that place Massah Umeribah (Testing and Quarrel) because of the quarrel of the Israelites and their testing of God; for they said, "Is God in our midst or not?" (Exod. 17:1–7)

Quite literally Moses slaps the rock at Mount Horev with his stick. There at the mountain also known as Sinai, he once again raises the miraculous staff that he used so effectively against Pharaoh and Egypt. There he has returned following the Exodus to the very site where God gave him his commission. There he smites the rock and brings forth water for a thirsting Israel. There, where he will receive the Ten Commandments, Moses settles the ugly display of doubt and petulance of the Israelites toward the God who redeemed them from slavery. At God's command, Moses slakes their thirst with a gush of water and yet another miracle. The Israelites quaff to their pleasure, unaware that they have provoked the displeasure of Moses and God.

Massah Umeribah becomes a byword for Israel's dangerous disloyalty. Thirst drives them to intemperate comments, which, in turn, provoke Moses' anger. He reads them well, I suspect, when he avers that they will soon stone him rather than simply whine at him. He also deflects their wrath by interpreting their anger toward him as anger toward God. No doubt he is correct, but his articulation of the displacement is, perhaps, impolitic. By absolutely identifying his leadership with God he humbly effaces himself, it is true. But in obviating his role as intermediary, he leaves Israel little room to release their anger at him rather than at God. Just as Moses will later play the role of prophet as he intercedes for Israel to God and so deflects God's wrath from them, here he could have accepted their blame and so deflected their rage at God. Better to anger a fellow human than to incur the wrath of the Master of the Universe.

But Moses is only too human, he does not easily endure the incessant carping and whining. God offers Moses an expedient that allows him to discharge his own anger at the Israelites for their inability to cope with thirst even for a moment. Moses takes up the cudgel and smites the rock. His anger discharged, the rock discharges water for the Israelites. Everyone seems happy, but we have witnessed a serious failure of Moses' leadership. It is a failure that, when repeated, will cost him dearly. Moses has yet to fathom the slave mentality of the Israelites. He never endured the lash. He never hungered or thirsted. He never was so defenseless that the whining of the perennial victim seemed to be his only recourse.

Moses may have been fit to represent God in Pharaoh's court, his own years as a courtier so qualified him. But he could not lead Israel well without brother Aaron at his side. The irony of Exodus is that Moses believed that he needed Aaron to be his spokesman to Pharaoh. In reality, he needed Aaron, who had been enslaved, to establish his bona fides to the Israelites. When Moses stands on his own as leader, he has no patience for these slaves. He remains the disdainful courtier, a patrician unsympathetic to pangs of thirst that send them delirious with fear. His anger toward the Israelites' wretched simpering combines disastrously with his insistence on identifying his leadership with God's. Humility and temper undermine his leadership of the Jews.

If we but add a dose of loss, of personal sorrow to this mix, Moses is set for a failure that will haunt him to his dying day. The biblical book of Numbers, chapter twenty, provides the occasion. We must read carefully to distinguish that story from this one we have just read in Exodus. They are very similar—much like the two versions of the quail story we saw in the previous chapter of this book. But the differences between the first incident of water at Meribah and the second incident, which we will now read, determine Moses' fate all the way up to the top of Mount Nebo, many years down the road.

> The Israelites, the entire confederation, came to the wilderness of Zin . . . and Miriam died and was buried there. There was no water for the federated tribes and they assembled against Moses and against Aaron. The people quarreled with Moses, saying, "Would that we had expired when our brethren did so before God! Why have you taken the congregation of God to this wilderness so that we and our beasts should die there? Why did you bring us up from Egypt to bring us to this evil place? It is not cultivated with figs or vines or pomegranates; there is no water to drink!"

Moses and Aaron went from the mob to the entrance of the tent of assembly. There they fell to their faces when the glory of God appeared to them. God said to Moses, "Take your staff and gather the confederation—you and your brother Aaron—and before their eyes speak to the rock so that it give forth its water. You will bring forth water from the rock and water the confederation and their beasts."

So Moses took his staff from God's presence, as God had commanded him. Moses and Aaron gathered the mob before the rock and he said to them, "Listen, O you rebels. Can we draw water from this rock for you?" Then Moses raised his hand and struck the rock twice with his staff. Copious water gushed forth and the confederation and their beasts drank.

Then God said to Moses and Aaron, "Because you did not trust in Me to sanctify Me before the eyes of the Israelites, thus you shall not bring this congregation into the land that I have given them."

Those were the waters of Meribah, where the Israelites quarreled with God, who was sanctified in them.

It should be clear that this story in the book of Numbers (20:1–13) closely parallels the story of Exodus (17:1–7), which we read at the outset of this chapter. The differences between the stories are so few, in fact, as to invite speculation that they are two versions of the same event. Yet the rabbinic readers of these stories are careful to distinguish between the two accounts. For those readers of old it is what changes in the two tellings that accounts for the severe reprimand and punishment God gives to Moses and Aaron. But before we discuss those differences we need to add one more passage to the discussion, for it effectively sandwiches the Numbers account of the water of Meribah between two events of the utmost personal importance to Moses. These events are necessary backdrop for understanding what went wrong between Moses and God, as well as between Moses and Israel.

The Numbers story just above comprises verses 20:1–13, ten verses later we read:

God spoke to Moses and to Aaron at Mount Hor, on the border of Edom, "Aaron shall be gathered to his people, for he shall not go

into the land I have given to the Israelites, because you quarreled
with my word at the waters of Meribah. Take Aaron and his son
Elazar and have them ascend Mount Hor. Let Aaron remove his
garments and clothe his son Elazar in them. Then Aaron shall
be gathered in and die there. So Moses did as God commanded
him . . . and Aaron died there atop the mountain. Moses and
Elazar descended from the mountain and the congregation saw
that Aaron had died. The entire house of Israel wept for Aaron
thirty days.

We see now that the incident at Meribah is bracketed by the
deaths of Moses' two older siblings. It is interesting to note what the
Bible tells us and what information it withholds. We have not heard
any word of Moses' parents since his birth, feeding, and subsequent
weaning. I do not think we would be far wrong if we presumed that
they had perished under the harsh slavery in Egypt, either during
the years Moses was growing up in Pharaoh's court or during the
years that Moses was a fugitive in Midian. Nowhere have we seen
Moses mourn the loss of his birth parents, Amram and Yocheved.
For that matter, neither have we seen Moses mourn the apparent
loss of his adoptive mother, the daughter of Pharaoh. As for his
adoptive grandfather, who perhaps was a surrogate father to him,
the only emotion we might have imagined for Moses was relief at his
passing. You will remember that after Moses struck the Egyptian
taskmaster and killed him for beating an Israelite, "grandpa"
Pharaoh sought to kill Moses in turn. Only when he learned of the
Pharaoh's death did Moses return to Egypt to free the Jews from the
new Pharaoh.

Moses is a complex character here, bereft of two sets of parents,
both of whom have passed apparently unmourned. Further, his feelings toward both sets of parents are of necessity baroque. The "parents" who raised him are the enemy. Moses surely had a fondness for
the family that raised him in the palace, but we have already seen
how he broke with them. If he is resolute about the Pharaoh who
acted the role of (grand)father, he may not have fully worked out his
loss of the "mother" who drew him from the river and gave him a
life no Israelite could even imagine. What happened to her when he
fled to Midian? Where was she when he returned to free the Jews?

Is she yet alive wondering about her Moses? If so, does he ever miss her? Does Moses regret the loss of his adoptive mother to the demands of God and Israel?

Moses may have tender memories from his earliest childhood of his birth parents, Amram and Yocheved, but perhaps he has no memories at all. In any case, how would he remember them: as parents who saved his life or as parents who abandoned him to adoption? If the former, does he feel guilty that they saved him and now he lives while they died miserably as slaves? This is a syndrome that many Holocaust survivors endure—the guilt that comes with the unrepayable debt.

If, on the other hand, he resents that they have "abandoned" him, there may still be residual guilt at his own survival. He need not search for his birth parents, he knows who they are. He has surviving siblings of those parents to fill him in on family history. Having "found" those siblings, he has recovered his "lost" family. I've been heading toward Miriam and Aaron all along. I think that to understand Moses at this essential juncture in his life, we must try to analyze his relationships with his older siblings. I suspect that they served as yet a third set of parents to Moses. Given the responsibility he carried every day in his leadership of Israel and his intermediation between the Israelites and God, and given the apparent absence of his wife, Tzipporah, and sons from the Egyptian scene, his siblings must have played an enormous role in Moses' life. The support they offered may in fact have been essential to his well-being as a leader.

Aaron's death is accounted for in some detail, with sympathy and even a touch of pathos. We will not dwell here on the difficulties that Aaron endured in his own life—not only his youthful slavery but the death of his two eldest sons, which is spelled out elsewhere in the Torah—suffice it to say that his life is worthy of a long, tragic novel. We should remark that his death is mourned by both Moses and Israel. A full thirty-day mourning period is observed for Aaron following his death on Mount Hor.

Of course, his death presages Moses' own death on Nebo. Each brother is commanded by God to climb to the mountaintop and give up the ghost. But Aaron's death is preceded by the ceremony of handing the mantle, quite literally, to his surviving son, Elazar. Elazar must be full of foreboding, he has already witnessed the deaths of his two elder brothers, Nadav and Avihu. Elazar must, then, also have some sympathy for his uncle Moses, he knows what it is like to lose a brother.

Yet Aaron is not just any brother, not even any big brother. It was Aaron who spoke Moses' words to Pharaoh. It was Aaron who alongside Moses performed the plagues that freed the Jews from servitude in Egypt. It was Aaron who served as the first high priest of the people Israel. As God told Moses "Aaron will be your prophet." Every would-be Johnson needs his Boswell, and Aaron was so for Moses. Or perhaps it would be more apropos to say that Boswell was Johnson's Aaron.

The congenial host of my Exodus study group offered a great deal of insight into the Moses-Aaron dynamic. He is in his mid-forties and manages a large family real estate company in New York. His younger brother works side by side with him—they actually share a very large desk in their mid-Manhattan office. He explained that it is often the case that he and his brother discuss a real estate deal and then act upon it. When they do so, however, the younger brother delivers the message in the older brother's name. "It makes me seem more powerful when he speaks in my name. It's like I'm behind the curtain, pulling the strings. We both look stronger." I have also observed that, as a result of this peculiar business arrangement, there seems to be genuine love and respect between two brothers who are in each other's face every working day. Though Aaron was the older brother, he did the same for Moses as these brothers in real estate do for each other. And, like them, there seems to have been genuine love and respect flowing between Moses and Aaron.

But Aaron plays an even more complex role. He is Moses' link to family history and Jewish tradition. The older brother serves as a mentor to Moses and helps him reconnect to the Israelite traditions he had left behind when he moved first to Pharaoh's court and then on to Midian. It is Aaron who must do the explaining to Moses about who's who in the tribes, who are the movers and shakers, who the complainers, who can safely be ignored, and who need be attended to. It may well be Aaron who reminds Moses what he learned as an infant on his mother's knee (and surely also heard from Miriam), that they were Jews, descendants of Abraham, Isaac, Jacob, and Joseph, and destined to inherit the Promised Land of

Canaan. It is appropriate that Aaron plays high priest to Moses' role as prophet. Aaron faithfully carries on the traditions, reads his lines, performs the rituals that bind them to God. Moses, for his part, innovates, comes from the outside with a new vision, speaks and acts for justice and righteousness in the name of God.

When Aaron dies Israel loses a trusted leader. Moses loses the older brother whom he loves and who for so much of his life did not have. The loss of Aaron must seem a bitter blow to Moses, as bitter as the waters of Marah. In losing Aaron he loses a buddy, a spokesman, a traditionalist, a political adviser, and a brother who most likely stood in loco parentis. It is good that Moses had a full thirty days to bid his brother farewell, to mourn for him and recognize that the loss has changed him.

How much harder then was it for Moses to lose his big sister, Miriam. Thanks to my own, I am fully aware of the tendencies of big sisters to act the role of mother, whether you want them to or not. I am certain that Moses must have found Miriam's tendency to mother him somewhat annoying at first, as I used to. But since the death of my own mother I appreciate that my sister is willing to stand in that role. It both reassures me and saves me from playing the role for myself. I suspect that, in time, Moses, too, came to appreciate that Miriam acted as the mom. It hearkens all the way back to the rabbis imagining that the midwives, way back at the outset of Exodus, could have been Yocheved and Miriam. It seems that even the rabbis of old had big sisters and could easily imagine the big sister, Miriam, acting in tandem with the mother to fill the role of nurturer-midwife.

Miriam was more than midwife to Moses, she saved his life when he was a baby. It was she who followed the basket down the Nile to be sure it was safe. It was she who suggested to Pharaoh's daughter that Yocheved act the wet-nurse and so brought baby Moses back home. It was she who first stood with him in the Nile and it was she who stood with him at the shore of the Reed Sea to sing the song of praise to God, their Deliverer. It was Miriam the prophet who prepared her little brother for his role as prophet—she led the path for her baby boy.

Moses' sense of debt to Miriam must have been as powerful as his love for his protective older sister. Whether near or far she constantly watched out for him. Not a day went by that Moses did not keenly appreciate all that his sister had done for him. In his heart, Moses knew that it could have as easily been she as he standing with Aaron before Pharaoh, were such things done in those days. It must have been especially pleasing when Moses saw Miriam receive recognition as a prophet at the shores of the sea following Israel's miraculous crossing. In many ways his sister, who like Aaron was absent for too much of his adult life, stood in the breach for him as surrogate mother after Yocheved and then Pharaoh's daughter each had died. It was Miriam who provided the ease of female companionship when he was bereft of his wife, Tzipporah, during his epic battle with Pharaoh. Even when Miriam gossiped about him, he stood up for his older sibling. Like many baby brothers who grow up, Moses grew protective of his big sister.

How heartbreaking, then, that Miriam's death is recorded en passant, so minimally in the Numbers narrative of the events at Meribah. We are told nothing more than Miriam died and was buried there. It is as though her importance to Israel's history, her role as leader of Israel's women, her centrality as Moses' sister are all washed away by the bitter quarrel between Moses, God, and Israel at Meribah. By now biblical readers have sadly grown used to the strong women of Israel being given short shrift in the Israelite history. Her heroic actions during Pharaoh's persecutions go unmentioned at her death. Her Song at the Sea goes unsung as funereal hymn. Her saving of Moses goes unrecognized as her brother is forced to deal with the outrageous argument of the Israelites against God. It would be easy for Moses to feel that those damn slaves had again stolen his sister from him. The burdens of leadership weighed more heavily than ever on Moses as they denied him room for the heavy weight of mourning his sister, his protector, his Miriam.

The Bible records no tears shed for Miriam, no passing of the mantle of prophecy or even of the tambourine she used to lead the women in song. The Bible does not tell us of Moses' grief, his sitting with Aaron to remember their beloved Miriam. Nowhere do we read of Moses pouring out his grief for his motherly big sister, and possibly using that occasion to also finally mourn Yocheved, Amram, even Pharaoh's daughter. So many unshed tears as the biblical account hurriedly turns to the brewing rebellion of the Israelites, once again at the site of the waters of Massah Umeribah. It is as though, once there, they could only test God and quarrel. Even in the wilderness of Sinai, as my real estate study partners would teach me, location is everything.

So Israel repeats the scene at Meribah, once again whining about water and bitching that they were better off in Egypt. Once again God calls upon Moses to placate their thirst for water with strong leadership. Once again Moses gathers the elders and proceeds to the rock at Horev. God commands Moses and Aaron to sanctify God's name, speak to the rock, and bring forth water. But Moses and Aaron, so bent by their mourning for Miriam, are bent only on repeating the previous Meribah performance. They just go through the routine by rote—something that must have been a constant temptation to Aaron in his role as priest. Now, in their suppressed mourning for Miriam, they go through the motions at Meribah, not attending to a subtle but essential detail in God's command.

God commands that they speak to the rock, but instead, in their grief, Moses does as he had been bidden to do before. He raises his staff, the very staff turned serpentine to prove his case to Israel and Pharaoh, the staff that turned the Nile to blood, the staff that cleft the sea and left the Israelites singing on dry land, and with that staff, which had once before brought water from the rock, he smites the rock again and again.

The water that gushes forth is as copious as Moses' unshed tears for Miriam might have been. It is as though the waters that pour forth show us how Moses has acted out in anger, unable to hear God clearly because of his grief. It is a very dangerous lapse to be in the presence of God and not give God one's full attention. As the rabbis of old are fond of pointing out, there are two things that distort the normal order of life: love and grief. Moses has an abundance of each of these for his dead sister, Miriam.

God reacts immediately to the lapse in attention that Moses and Aaron have committed. Though it was Moses who struck the rock, Aaron stood with him as an accomplice. Each was guilty of not distinguishing a nuance of God's command—and it was a nuance that, though subtle, was telling. Had they spoken to the rock and water gushed forth, how much would God's power have been glorified and sanctified. Those troublesome Israelites had once before had their thirst slaked at Meribah when Moses struck the rock and yet they still had not learned that God would provide. Was not an even greater miracle called for to convince them? But Moses did not heed the exigencies of the situation, so immersed was he in his own grief for Miriam. And Aaron, master of ritual detail in his role as high priest, somehow also ignores this essential change of rite.

So God exacts punishment from the bewildered brothers. Each is informed that now they will not enter the Promised Land. Aaron can no longer function as high priest under these circumstances, his priesthood is passed on, his life comes to a close. Moses is informed of the fate that we have witnessed for him in the very first chapter of this book, a glimpse of the Promised Land from atop Mount Nebo, and then his own death. Each brother ascends to the top of his own mountain, but neither steps foot in the Promised Land.

But still, the infraction they committed seems minor compared to the burdens and devotions both brothers have offered to God. One might expect a bit of mercy, some sympathy from the Master of the Universe for two brothers mired in grief. Surely one small lapse merits some forgiveness, doesn't it? A punishment of exile and death seems so extreme. Does it not count for God that Moses is God's prophet?

I think Moses' grief here is only part of his undoing. Already in the Exodus incident at Meribah we saw that Moses had identified so closely with God that he would not take the heat of Israel's rebellion upon himself. He feared getting stoned rather than fearing that Israel might provoke God's wrath. It is Moses' job as prophet to intercede for Israel. Instead, he blames Israel before God in a moment of tired frustration. His own anger then puts God and Israel at risk. God is at risk of blasphemy—for they ask "Is God in our midst or not?" Israel is at risk of annihilation when God reacts to the blasphemy. Moses does not merely ignore a minor detail; it is not simply that he hits the rock instead of speaking to it. The striking of the rock is emblematic of Moses' self-absorption. He forgets that the prophet must be at risk himself. The prophet must endure both God's wrath and Israel's scorn if he is to succeed in his role as intercessor.

It is hard not to have sympathy for Moses. He has lost a sister who was like a mother to him. Can he not be allowed an error in his moment of grief? And could Israel not refrain from pressing him with their needs when they saw him enveloped by his own human needs? How high is the price of leadership that a man cannot mourn his sister, his mother, his father? Can there be no private solace for the public leader? Can he not withdraw for a brief moment to shed his tears?

Here we also see that if Israel is childlike in their demands upon Moses, God is a jealous God who brooks no competition. Just as Pharaoh is destroyed for his hubris in presuming worship of Egypt for himself, Moses is punished for turning his devotion away from the details of God's commandments and toward his mourning of Miriam. It is as though God and God alone will play the role of surrogate parent to Moses. God appears to expect that Moses should have only God to turn to. Can it be that God is jealous of Moses' need for Miriam? Might this account for the severity of God's reaction to both Moses and Aaron? If they deny God the right to play the role of comforter to them upon the loss of Miriam, then God will deny them, too.

This is not a pretty picture of God. We expect God to be merciful, beneficent, nurturing, warm and cuddly, parental. But if Exodus has taught us anything, it is that we must be as wary as the Egyptians themselves at putting another in the role God means to play. Clergy have long advocated that God comforts mourners. It is a role I believe is useful—even if the comfort is derived by projecting anger at the God who is Master of life and death. It is a useful outlet for human psychology, for when God plays this role the anger that humans feel in the face of death is not directed at other humans who suffer the same loss. It is a role I think that is normally a useful one for God to play in the mourning process, for even in anger it maintains a relationship between the mourner and God.

But in his own moment of mourning, Moses did not have the privilege of personal anger at God. Quite the contrary, his role was to deflect anger *from* God. Moses did not do so and Israel blasphemed. In the words of Numbers, God says to Moses, "you did not trust in Me to sanctify Me before the eyes of the Israelites." Moses failed God as prophet to Israel. Moses failed Israel as leader and intercessor. Perhaps Moses even failed Miriam for not understanding that his role as prophet demanded that he submerge his mourning for her and lead the Israelites. They, too, had suffered loss. They, too, mourned the death of their surrogate mother. At the very moment when one of their prophets was taken from them, their other prophet, Moses, did not intercede. Instead he let his anger overtake him and the waters of Meribah flowed.

In indulging his suppressed anger, Moses failed himself. He ceased to attend to God's saving commands and so lost an opportunity for succor and support following his loss of Miriam. The end was that he suffered the further loss of Aaron. At that moment Moses understood that his failure of leadership indeed precluded him from crossing the Jordan and entering the Promised Land.

For his part, Aaron dies on Mount Hor, never even having seen the Promised Land. But Aaron is given the solace of passing the mantle to his son, Elazar. It is no coincidence that the name of that son means "God helps." Moses and Aaron looked to Miriam and when she was lost to them failed to look to God for help. In ignoring the essential details of God's command they missed the chance to sanctify God and bring holiness to their own lives at a moment when they were desperate for it. Instead, Moses despaired and struck out. The very symbol of God's help became an instrument of anger.

Ironically, God shows mercy to Moses at the very moment of his punishment—that is if knowing the circumstances of one's death can be considered a mercy. We are inclined to wonder how our lives will end, and I think Moses was no less immune to this speculation than anyone else. As a result of the incidents at Meribah, God informs Moses that he will not enter the Promised Land. If Moses is capable of reasoning by analogy from what happens to Aaron, he may infer that he, too, will have a moment on a mountaintop, a peak moment if you will, and then expire. However much reassurance that offers, it is all God gives Moses as a sop for his punishment.

It is not clear from the context whether Moses is inclined to receive this as a tender gesture from the stern Lord who metes out such severe punishment. He must now not only mourn his sister's death, but soon on its heels his brother's death as well. Moses has no parent to rely on any longer but his Father in Heaven. Thrown back upon that relationship, one that he first came to depend on during his years shepherding in the same Sinai wilderness, Moses finds the strength to continue leading the Israelites. His thirst for God grows, and he teaches the Jews to share that desire. If only he could teach them to crave God as they hungered for water at Meribah. As for himself, Moses now knows the end of the story, as do we. But the road still wants walking, the mountain still needs to be climbed, and battles must still be fought.

MEMORANDUM:
KILL THE
BASTARDS

So Amalek came and battled the Israelites at Rephidim. Moses told Joshua, "Select for us some men and go do battle against Amalek. Tomorrow I will station myself at the top of the hill with the staff of the Lord in my hand."

Joshua did battle with Amalek as Moses had told him, while Moses, Aaron, and Hur ascended to the top of the hill. It came to pass that whenever Moses would raise his arms, Israel would prevail, while if he lowered his arms, Amalek would prevail. Moses' arms grew heavy, so they took a rock and placed it beneath him and he sat upon it. Aaron and Hur supported his arms, one on each side, so that his hands were steady until sunset. Joshua weakened Amalek and his people with the sword.

God said to Moses, "Write this as a memorandum in a scroll and make it be heard by Joshua: I will utterly wipe out any memory of Amalek from beneath the heavens."

Moses built an altar and called it "God Is My Battle-Flag." He said, "I vow by the throne of God: War against Amalek for God from generation to generation!" (Exod. 17:8–16)

The war of Amalek comes as a shock in our story. We grew complacent, as did Israel. We thought, with them, that the fighting was over. We expected that the only fighting we would see would be the bickering between God, Moses, and Israel for the next forty years of wandering in the wilderness. Suddenly, the tribe of Amalek is on the scene and the alarm is raised. Israel must once again battle her enemies. While this may have the salutary effect of unifying the tribes against outside forces, it comes at the cost of lives and the terror that ensues. Israel's security is shaken. They had thought that the only terror that the wilderness held for them was their own slave-bred terror about food and drink for the morrow. Instead, swords and lances clash around them.

The mid-second-century Rabbi Joshua ben Qorkha imagines that the battle of Amalek comes as a direct response to Israel's perfidious blasphemy of God about which we read in the last chapter. There, you will recall, they whined to God and Moses, again, about water. They actually said they were better off in Egypt. Even after the miraculous defeat of Pharaoh's forces, they wondered aloud whether God could still be on their side. As Rabbi Joshua imagined it: "They said: God has abandoned us in the wilderness. God's Presence is no longer among us. As it is written, 'Is God in our midst or not?' So what comes following this chapter of the Bible? 'So Amalek came...' Amalek came upon them to punish them!"

For Rabbi Joshua, Amalek repays Israel's perfidy. His senior colleague, a rabbi named Elazar from the town of Modiin, explained that those sneaky Amalekites were perfidious in their turn. According to Rabbi Elazar, Amalek would slither in under cloud cover and steal away with Israelites, killing them out of earshot. As a proof, Rabbi Elazar refers to the story of the battle of Amalek as it is told in the last of the Five Books of Moses, Deuteronomy (25:17–19), where Moses commands the Israelites: "'Remember what Amalek did to you on the road during the Exodus from Egypt. How he came upon you on the road and sneaked up upon all those falling behind in the rear, when you were tired and weary—and did not fear God. . . . Wipe out any memory of Amalek from beneath the heavens. Do not forget!'"

Rabbi Elazar makes a perceptive comment on the middle verse. He suggests that the clause "and did not fear God" does not refer to the cowardly Amalekites who attacked the stragglers, but to the Israelites themselves. Not only is it a grammatically plausible reading, but Rabbi Elazar's point is well taken. Those ungrateful Israelites who doubted that God's presence was among them should hardly expect to rely on God's protection. If they believe God is absent, so be it; they will then be at the mercy of their enemies—even those as lowly and sneaky as Amalek who mount terrorist attacks on the helpless. It will be up to Moses to rally the Israelites to God and remind them of the efficacy of God's presence. Only then, when they recognize God among them, can they defeat Amalek.

It is precisely this interpretation that is given by Rabbi Elazar and Rabbi Joshua's contemporaries when they read the passage from a slightly different angle but still arrive at the same conclusion. Many of the earliest commentaries on the battle of Amalek worry about Moses' role in the battle. We will study this concern below, but first an aside is needed to fill in the background to this particular rabbinic approach. There are those rabbis who see Moses as setting a good example. They comment on Moses' command to Joshua, "Select for us some men . . ." They point out that the phrase "for us" is superfluous to the verse. It could just as well have read, "Select some men"; in fact, that is precisely how I first translated it, but then revised my free rendering of the Hebrew in favor of a more literal reading. Why "for us"? Because, the rabbis of the second century comment, by including Joshua in "us," Moses displays good leadership qualities. Joshua now feels invested; he has a stake in the outcome of the battle. He has been equated with Moses in that word *us*. At that moment Joshua steps into the ranks of leadership of Israel. Imagine, Moses referred to him using the word *us*!

A full millennium after this commentary, a twelfth-century midrash on the passage goes a step farther in praising Moses' canny leadership. Not only has he made Joshua feel included, but Moses has prepared him for his future. The battle of Amalek is Joshua's debut in Scripture, until now his name has not been mentioned. But we readers of the Bible know that it will be Joshua who will lead the next generation of Israelites to cross the Jordan and conquer the Promised Land. Joshua will be Moses' successor, but he will essentially exercise his leadership of Israel through his capacity as a general. Indeed, the book of the Bible that follows the Five Books of Moses is named Joshua, and charts his exploits. What better way for Moses to induct him into military rank than to test his mettle under fire. His first assignment is essentially a skirmish, yet one that will be remembered throughout Israelite history, from generation to generation. Thus Moses counsels Joshua and trains him in the ways of war.

Moses is praised for yet another lesson he teaches during the battle of Amalek. As early as the second century it was noted that, during the battle, Moses' physical stamina was essential for the prosecution of the engagement. When he tired, his aides-de-camp sat him on a rock to give his aging body some of the physical support he required to endure. The rabbis ask, "Wasn't there a pillow or a cushion for him to sit on that they had to put a rock under him?" The question is sympathetic to Moses' derriere, but it is also rhetorical. The rabbis answer their own question, "Moses himself requested the rock and said, So long as the Israelites are being discomfited, I, too, will be uncomfortable." The rabbis conclude, "Blessed is the person who feels the people's pain with them." Obviously some sages are of the opinion that a leader who can "feel your pain" is a great leader. For others, perhaps, that sharing of pain is nothing more than what it looks like: a pain in the ass.

Of course, the rabbinic question and answer displayed here is the very hallmark of their dialectic style. It brings me back to the trouble they had with the story of the battle of Amalek in the first place. Their worry about Moses' role in the battle is not only out of solicitude for his tender tushy. The rabbis do not like the implications of the story. As they ask it, "Since when do Moses' arms make or break a war?"

This is no idle question. It just seemed too magical to the rabbis that Moses, stationed atop his hill, should be able to affect the battle by simply raising or lowering his arms. It would be one thing if he were up there gazing down on the battlefield from a good vantage point and, on the basis of the intelligence he gleaned, made decisions about the deployment of his troops. But the text is emphatic, whenever Moses would raise his arms Israel would prevail. If this were not mumbo jumbo enough for the rabbis, a medieval mystical text is horrified at the converse: When he lowered his arms, Amalek would prevail. "Could it be that Moses might affect victory for Amalek?" it shudders to ask.

The whole scene of Moses standing atop the hill with his arms out to his sides makes Jews edgy. We remember another famous Jew atop a hill, arms splayed, legs crossed at the ankles. The rabbis were reminded often enough of the crucified Jesus, particularly the image of the cross as a sign of militant Christianity, not to get nervous when the Torah seemed to hint at such a type scene. We need to be careful about history here, because the earliest rabbis I have quoted in this chapter lived in the mid-second century. Now we all know that Jesus was crucified in the early first century, but it is only fair to point out that the image of the cross as a symbol of Christian militance dates from the mid-fourth century. Only after the Church historian Eusebius spun the tale of the Emperor Constantine's dream (in which he saw a cross in the sky and the banner, "By this sign shall you be victorious") did the Jews get the creeps about Christian triumphalism. By then, however, it was too late; the Roman Empire was already a Christian empire.

Still, the early rabbis may be nervous nevertheless. It was not only military types who associated this scene with Jesus. As early as the nineties of the first century, the Church father Barnabas comments on this passage about Amalek by associating it with the cross. He suggests that the reason Moses puts his hands out that way is so readers know "they cannot be saved if they do not put their hope in Him." Barnabas also points to another passage of Scripture that to him teaches the same lesson of salvation. He quotes from Numbers 21, the passage that follows the story of Meribah and Aaron's death that we read in our last chapter. Since the rabbis of the second and third century also link this passage from Numbers 21 with the Exodus and Numbers stories about Amalek we are studying here, it is worth a brief detour.

There (Num. 21:4–9) we read:

> They traveled from Mount Hor . . . and the people were impatient
> on the road. The people spoke against God and Moses: "Why did
> you take us up from Egypt to die in the wilderness? There is neither
> bread nor water and we are impatient with this damned food
> [manna]."
>
> Then God sent viperous serpents upon the people. They bit the
> people and a large number of Israelites died. The people came to
> Moses and said, "We sinned when we spoke against God and you.
> Pray to God to remove these serpents from us." So Moses prayed on
> behalf of the people.
>
> God said to Moses, "Make a viper and place it on a standard. It
> will come to pass that anyone who is bitten and looks upon it will
> survive." So Moses made a bronze serpent and placed it on a
> standard. It came to pass that if a serpent had bitten a person, if he
> looked at the bronze serpent he survived.

Again, the first-century Church father Barnabas takes the serpent
on the standard as a type of allegory, symbolizing Jesus on the cross.
Looking at the standard causes Christians to hope on him and find
salvation. The rabbis, as I said above, also link this passage with the
Amalek passage. Of Moses at the battle of Amalek they asked,
"Since when do Moses' arms make or break a war?" In the case of
the bronze serpent they ask, "Since when does a serpent have the
power of life and death?" Again, the narrative is a bit too magical
for rabbinic comfort. Like Barnabas, they see the lesson of these stories as pointing beyond the immediate players. The answer to both
questions the rabbis ask is the same: "What this teaches is that when
the Israelites set their gaze upward and enlist their hearts to the service of their Father in Heaven, they are victorious."

This somewhat sappy interpretation of Moses' ostensible magic
makes us realize that when the rabbis imagined him sitting on his
rock on the hilltop, they did not see him with arms parallel to the
ground. On the contrary, in the rabbinic imagination, Moses was
seated with his arms reaching upward, directing the Israelites to cast
their gaze beyond him, heavenward. The posture of a supplicant
with arms upward was well known in the time of the rabbis. We

even have art from that period, frescoes that depict persons in this prayer posture. The synagogue of Dura-Europos has just such a fresco in which the elders of the twelve tribes of Israel each stand before their tents, arms raised as they pray for water in the wilderness. In the center of the fresco at Dura stands Moses, staff in hand, striking the rock to bring forth the answer to their prayers.

Now that we know how this episode of Amalek has been interpreted in rabbinic times, it behooves us to trace a bit of the Amalek tradition in earlier, biblical times. For the story of Amalek, the outside invader who preys on the weak and helpless of Israel, caught the Jewish imagination almost from the moment of their first foray. The story of Amalek was a symbol not only of God's protective presence but of Israel's vulnerability to outside attack. The accounts we have read in Exodus and in Deuteronomy make clear that Amalek is nothing but trouble as far as the Torah is concerned. Deuteronomy is especially hard on them, describing Amalek in the most cowardly terms.

It is, I suppose, a sign of Moses' leadership that he rallies the troops to defeat them. If, indeed, Amalek has come as the scourge of God to punish Israel for its inability to sustain faith, then Moses' actions on the hilltop go a long way to restoring both Israel's faith in God and the relationship between the people and God. The narrative itself gives an indication that the restoration of faith is Moses' goal; he realizes that if they have support, they can be shown God's presence among them still. In the Hebrew text, the weary Moses himself seeks support from Aaron and Hur. With each at his sides, his arms hold steady. The term I have translated as "steady" is unusual in this context. The Hebrew term is *emunah,* which normally is biblical Hebrew for steadfast faith. When the Israelites crossed the Reed Sea, they believed in God and in Moses. The term for their belief there shares the same Hebrew root as "steady" here. So, the very steadiness of Moses' upraised arms not only directs the Israelites to recognize that God will protect them but to believe and have faith in God's abiding presence.

If the early rabbis are right in their identification of Hur, Moses, too, is given a lesson in steadfastness and constancy. In the late second century a midrash on this passage says of Hur: "He was Miriam's son." Frankly, there is no way to know if this hunch is correct, but it leaves us with a lovely scene. Moses is supported on either side, as it were, by his brother and sister. If the Torah or the rabbis deemed it inappropriate for Miriam to appear in a scene of battle, they suggest that her son, Hur, was there at Moses' side offering his support. The only other place this Hur appears, he is again with Aaron when they accompany Moses onto Mount Sinai to receive the Torah. Hur himself becomes a symbol of steadfast and faithful family support at the significant moments of Moses' leadership of Israel.

As for Moses, he has overcome the failure of leadership that led him to strike the rock at Meribah. Instead, he directs Israel to God's saving presence. If this is not clear from the narrative, it is clear from his own battle cry, reified when Moses builds an altar to offer thanksgiving to the God who saved them from the onslaught of Amalek. "God is my Battle-Flag," Moses declares. His faith could have no more concrete expression.

The episode of Amalek ends with the curious vow that Moses takes, literally declaring, "My hand upon the throne of God!" What is it that Moses vows? "War against Amalek for God from generation to generation!" Since Joshua, with the help of Moses' intercession and God's aid, has decimated them by sword, we must wonder why Moses has such a ferocious sense of continuing vengeance against Amalek. Perhaps the nature of their attack, as described in the Deuteronomy account, requires such an overpowering response. But if Moses seems to have a powerful response to Amalek in Exodus, his response recorded in Deuteronomy is even more extreme. There, you will recall, he cries, "Remember what Amalek did to you on the road during the Exodus from Egypt. . . . Wipe out any memory of Amalek from beneath the heavens. Do not forget!" As I suggest in the title of this chapter, it is as though he dictates, Memorandum: Kill the bastards!

The memory of Amalek is no more easily eliminated from Jewish memory than is the memory of the Pharaoh who enslaved the Jews in Egypt. Yet of Pharaoh, Jews are commanded to remember, to tell, to reenact, and never to forget. Amalek is more curious, apparently a paradox. Moses commands the Jews to remember, he tells them not to forget Amalek. Yet they are not commanded to reenact the battle of Amalek. There is no Amalek seder. There are no special foods, like matzo, to eat. Instead, the reminder, the command is to wipe out any memory of the tribe. The very act of remembering to do so seems to preclude any possibility of wiping out Amalek's memory.

Indeed, if the Bible is any measure, Amalek will not be easily wiped out. The name Amalek appears some fifty times in Scripture, scattered from Genesis (where Amalek is listed as a descendant of evil Esau) through Exodus, Deuteronomy (which we've seen), on into the books of Judges (where they are curiously associated with the tribe of Moses' in-laws, the Midianites) and through the histories of the Israelite kings. In particular, Amalek figures in the reign of the first king, Saul. It is they who cause his downfall. Since Saul's loss of the kingship is a lesson in the failure of leadership, and like the case of Moses we saw in the last chapter, a lesson in what at first blush seems a minor infraction of God's command, it merits a closer inspection. How does Amalek persist in Jewish memory? How can the enemy be extirpated?

King Saul's undoing is a long story that involves not only himself and Amalek but a third character, the prophet Samuel. It is Samuel who anointed Saul king, and it will be Samuel who in God's name will remove Saul from the kingship for his failure to carry out God's commands about Amalek. It's a nasty, bloody tale, so sit back, read, enjoy.

> Samuel said to Saul, "Hear now the sound of the words of God. Thus says the God of hosts: 'I recall what Amalek did to Israel, how he set upon him on the road during the exodus from Egypt. Go now, strike Amalek, destroy-for-Me all that is his. Have no mercy upon him, kill every man and woman, toddler and suckling, ox and sheep, camel and donkey!'"
>
> So Saul mustered the people . . . and Saul came upon the city Amalek . . . and Saul struck Amalek . . . and captured Agag, king of Amalek, alive, but all the people he destroyed-for-God by the sword. But Saul and the people showed mercy to Agag and to the best of the sheep and cattle . . . and did not destroy-them-for-God, but all that was of no value and weak they destroyed-for-God.
>
> The word of God came to Samuel, saying, "I regret that I made Saul king, for he has turned from Me and not fulfilled My commands." . . .

When Samuel came to Saul, Saul greeted him, "Blessed be you by God, I have fulfilled God's command."

But Samuel responded, "But what is that bleating of sheep in my ears and the lowing of cattle I can hear?"

Saul replied, "We brought them from Amalek, for the people had mercy on the best of the sheep and cattle in order to sacrifice them to the Lord your God. The rest we destroyed-for-God."

Samuel said, ". . . Though you may seem small in your own eyes, God has anointed you king of Israel. God set you on the road and commanded you to go destroy-for-God those sinners, Amalek, do battle with them until you have extinguished them. Why did you not heed the command of God? Why did you swoop upon the spoil and so do what is evil in God's eyes? . . . Does God want burnt offerings and sacrifices or obedience to God's command? Indeed, obedience is better than sacrifices, paying attention is better than the fat of rams! . . . Because you have rejected God's word, God has rejected you as king!" . . .

Then Samuel said, "Bring me Agag, king of Amalek." They led Agag to him in chains . . . and Samuel cut down Agag before God. (1 Sam. 15)

Whew! Samuel the prophet is one tough cookie. He delivers the verdict of God to King Saul as unflinchingly as a parent berates a teenage child for not doing his or her chore of washing the dishes. Then, like the parent who takes the sponge in hand to do the neglected washing up, Samuel takes up the sword and lops off the head of Agag, king of Amalek. The ferociousness of the prophet Samuel is matched only by the insistence of God. The relentless dual demands of God for obedience and the destruction of Amalek flow throughout the Samuel-Saul narrative. The story we just read has its intensity mitigated for one brief moment of humor—a moment I fear gets lost in the translation. King Saul has been commanded to kill everything, everything. Men, women, children, cattle, sheep, everything. Yet he relents. Perhaps he follows modern military strategy that avoids "decapitation," which is to say: Do not kill off the opposing general, otherwise there will be no enemy leader to instruct the antagonist to stand down. But King Saul also spares cattle and sheep, intending to offer the best of the enemy flock as a sacrifice to God.

Let us assume the best of intentions for King Saul. Let us also assume that he sees a distinction between killing cattle on a battle-field and killing them solemnly at an altar as a dedicated offering to God. Meaning not disobedience but rather intending to carry out the spirit of God's command, King Saul spares the best oxen and sheep. This is his undoing. When the prophet Samuel appears in the military camp, he is incensed that Saul so blithely has ignored the letter of God's law. When King Saul protests, Samuel asks him, "But what is that bleating . . ." Here is the joke. I translate "but what," for one Hebrew word, a standard interrogative. I used the "but what" to try and capture the wordplay of the Hebrew, albeit poorly. What Samuel asks King Saul about the sheep is clever for its ono-matopoeic flair. Samuel has imitated the sheep themselves when he turns to Saul and interrogates him with that one Hebrew word, *meh*. He may as well have dismissed Saul's intended sacrifice as humbug and said, Bah!

For all of its humor, neither Samuel nor Saul were laughing. Samuel represents God's rage at being disobeyed by none less than the anointed king of Israel. God demands complete obedience in every detail, and this demand is framed with the clear possibility that the king of Israel must perform to a higher standard than a commoner. Samuel berates Saul, "though you may seem small in your own eyes . . . God set you on the road and commanded you . . . why did you not heed the command of God?" This may well be the appropri-ate heuristic for understanding Moses' failure about which we read in the preceding chapter. Leadership *does* demand a higher standard.

What intrigues me about this lesson is the way in which rabbinic Judaism has interpreted it. It is well illustrated by the story of a rab-binical school that, with pretensions to Ivy League status, decided to float a crew team. They bought a shell, found eight strong students to row, and yet one more to act the coxswain. Sadly, the crew lost every race they entered. Finally exasperated, the rabbi-coach sent the coxswain off to spy on Harvard's crew to learn the secret of their success. The boy came back from his mission perplexed. He reported, "At Harvard, eight of them row and apparently only one guy shouts directions."

This joke of "too many chiefs" has its upside in Jewish practice. Since everybody pretends to leadership, Jewish law treats everyone equally as a leader. The rabbi is no better, no step above in the hierarchy, no closer to God, no more bound by commandments. All Jews are leaders, thus all have demands upon them for a higher standard. This is the lesson the rabbis learn from both the stories of Moses and Saul. Everybody better pay close attention to the details of God's demands upon the Jews. Each individual bears the burdens of leadership for the entire community. It is up to each person whether Israel succeeds or fails, wins the war or loses. Each Jew is responsible for every other Jew in the community. Though you may seem small in your own eyes, God has anointed you king of Israel.

Here the lessons of leadership spread from Moses to the Jews as a people. At the battle with Amalek, the Israelites learn again to trust in Moses and feel God's protective presence among them. Their very victory in the guerrilla war teaches them that God has not abandoned them. Perhaps it is equally salutary for them to have seen Moses punished for his own disobedience, however minor, just as they have been punished. At this moment the Israelites are forced to notice that Moses stands up for them—to God and to Amalek. It is because of Moses that God defeats Amalek and Israel survives. In that moment the Jews finally identify with Moses. We, too, could be standing there, they think. We, too, could affect victory for all of Israel. We, too, are leaders. Joshua, one of us, was addressed by Moses with "us." We reciprocate and now recognize Moses as "us."

He who had been born among the Israelites but lived a life apart from them, he who had been raised in the palace of Pharaoh while Israel was enslaved, he who wandered free as a shepherd while they bent their backs under the lash, he, Moses, was now recognized as a fellow Israelite. At that moment, they all felt that God's presence was among them. When they enlisted themselves to service of God, to fight alongside Moses, they were victorious. Finally, they could relax enough to row while Moses shouted at them. The Jews had become a crew.

It is not merely coincidental, of course, that this transformation took place in the face of outside oppression. It is true they had faced the same under Egypt. But there the Jews were slaves. Once free, which is to say free to bicker with one another, they had an entirely new set of skills to master—the skills of peoplehood. The lessons had been taught repeatedly, but only now, with Amalek raging around them, were the lessons finally learned. Perhaps this is the reason that Amalek's oppression is to be recalled in every generation. The act of erasing Amalek's memory serves simultaneously to form Israel's identity. When Moses makes his vow to war against Amalek, it is possible that he is making a wish: Would that there be an Amalek in every generation against whom we can unite. Would that it be an Amalek, who in the end was a minor distraction, and not be an Egypt, who enslaved us.

The command "do not forget" is, then, not only a command to remember the insidious encroachment of outsiders upon the vulnerable, but a command to understand that it is precisely such an attack that rallies the people to unity and belief in leadership. When the outsider is repulsed, God's presence is appreciated. This lesson of Jewish history has, of course, universal implications. It is the soft underbelly of all racial, religious, and national identity formation. The easiest way to rally a nation is to point to the outside oppressor, the other, the one who imperils the weak and defenseless among you. That other, who would invade your borders, hit you when you're down, take you by surprise, that is the one who teaches you what it means to be an Israelite, a patriotic American, a proud Afro-American, a loyal Iraqi, a Muslim fundamentalist, a West Bank settler.

The invocation of the enemy may be real, Amalek may indeed be at the door, there may well be terrorists out there. And, as Moses learns, it works to take the vow, to raise the standard, to fly the banner that God is on our side. It is an important if dangerous lesson of leadership for Moses to have learned. Particularly in light of his previous failure of leadership over a trifle, this enticement to demagoguery carries its own terrors. The ease with which a Jewish leader can brand some outside threat as "Amalek" and expect a unified response from the people is matched, alas, by the ease with which leaders of nations throughout history have reviled the Jews for the same purposes. The sword Moses has unsheathed against Amalek is decidedly two-edged.

Much later in the Bible the absurdity of this cry of "Amalek" to bring everyone into line is parodied in the Book of Esther. There, in a biblical book that is entirely farce, a harem romance is linked with an oriental courtier intrigue to produce the most wicked humor about the Jewish community up to the days of Lenny Bruce and Mel

Brooks. The bad guy, the evil courtier Haman, is given a genealogy that traces him back to Agag, whom you will recall from the story of Samuel and Saul was the king of Amalek who lost his head.

In the Book of Esther the Jews are rallied against the bad guys with the help of a sweet young thing who sacrifices herself for the Jewish community by spending an entire year having a makeover by Elizabeth Arden followed by marriage to the gentile king. If this isn't Jewish princess fantasy enough, the girl's uncle saves the king's life from a court intrigue. The Book of Esther follows a plot line worthy of the Marx brothers until the Jews are saved. When it is all over, the girl is not just queen for a day, she's firmly on the throne with her uncle as the prime minister.

Haman, descendant of Agag-who-was-the-former-king-of-Amalek, is impaled along with his ten sons. The Jews kill thousands of their enemies, but, the text is careful to inform us, they do not lay a hand on the spoils. Apparently they had learned from King Saul's mistakes. To complete the broad wink that indicates the farce, the storyteller taxes the reader to believe that, on the morrow, the Jews were permitted to repeat the slaughter of their enemies. The parodist, no doubt wary of the invocation of Amalek to justify another Israelite fantasy of retribution, has made the dangerous part of the lesson of Amalek clear. To his credit, God's name is nowhere invoked in the Hebrew Book of Esther.

From Exodus through Esther, the lessons of Amalek are complex but important. Amalek does remind us that there can be danger away from the center. When the people are doubtful of leadership and, worse, insecure that God's presence is among them, they are most vulnerable. Only when they recognize that God is there, with their leadership, among them, can the battle be won. Moses performs the most important leadership when he teaches them confidence in God's saving presence.

The dangers implicit in the story of Amalek are manifest throughout history. Yes, there will always be an enemy. But be careful to distinguish between the Pharaohs of history, those who would truly enslave you, and the Amaleks, who though they may attack are probably not fatal. The former must be opposed with all one's power. It is for this reason that the Exodus is annually reenacted. There is a seder. We are enjoined repeatedly to tell our children the story, to teach them the lessons of the Exodus. The latter, the Amaleks that offer temptations to demagoguery, they are meant to be forgotten. Jews get drunk on Purim, when the Book of Esther is recited. There may be no better antidote to the pretensions of a rabble-rouser than rendering the rabble impotent to do any real harm.

The lessons of leadership merit rehearsal as well. Moses finally succeeds as a leader when he has shown himself human, vulnerable like the Israelites to erring in the service of God. His greatness is that having been punished, he still stands fast as the one who rouses Israel to service of God. His humility is profound, for he does not prickle against God's chastisement but grows from it. In his growth, he also shows humility toward Israel. He invites Aaron and Hur, two men of the Israelite folk, to join him in engaging the battle. Further, Moses asks Joshua to take up the escutcheon and pick warriors to defend Israel. That Joshua is included in the ranks of Israelite leadership is clear when Moses addresses him and says "Select for us some men."

It is also clear from this invitation that Israel has entered the reality of history and nations. When they were fleeing Egypt and whined in fear of the pursuing Egyptian army, Moses silenced their cowardice with the reassurance that God would fight for them. Here, it is clear to Moses and to Israel that, again, God will fight for them. But they must join battle themselves. Moses tells Joshua, "Select for us some men and go do battle against Amalek." God will not perform miracles unless Israel participates in the war. Moses will not stand alone in the breach, either. Israel must commit men and matériel to the skirmish. They do so, and in cooperation with Moses and with faith in God, they prevail.

This is as important a lesson to Moses as it is to Israel. To the people it is clear that they must transform from dependent slaves to an independent and self-reliant people. Yes, God and Moses will stand with them. But it will now be Moses' job to lead *them,* with faith in God. Once they realize that they must take responsibility for themselves, they cease whining like small children and finally behave as adults. They take up the gauntlet and fight their own battle. Israel is reminded that even so, they cannot go it all alone, they must have partnership with God.

As for Moses, he learned long ago of the redeeming value of God's partnership. What he has learned in the battle of Amalek is that to forge a nation, he and God simply are not enough. Israel, too, must be included. He reaches out to the capable leadership, Joshua, and also relies on his family, Aaron and, perhaps, Hur. In turn, Joshua selects more leadership among the Israelites. Thus organized they can confront the enemy. The battle of Amalek is successful for it teaches Israel how to enter the realm of history when previously they had been utterly dependent on the realm of the supernatural. Now, not only God, but Israel partakes of responsibility in the relationship between them.

Dual responsibility for the two sides of relationship is the first step on the journey to covenant. Moses must learn and then educate Israel that he alone cannot be the only one in relationship with God. Israel must learn to fight for itself. But Israel must also learn how to relate to God without the intermediation of Moses. This step allows Moses the first glimpse of realizing that he can help affect the transformation from slavery to freedom. It is a relief, even as it is a consternation. Moses must fully apprehend that he cannot carry the nation alone.

Indeed, to be a nation, the mass of slaves must each become responsible members of a community. To succeed in leadership, Moses must learn to step away from leading. He has to appoint a successor, Joshua. Having a succession plan in place marks a milestone on Moses' own road to redemption. To become a nation, Israel must develop a broad base of leadership at every level of the tribal confederation. That is Moses' next great challenge.

FATHER
IN LAW

My father died during the summer after my first year of rabbinical school, just over twenty-five years ago. My mother is also gone, now more than half a decade. It makes me all the more appreciative of my in-laws, both father and mother-in. Despite all the jokes people tell to the contrary, I not only love my parents-in-law, but find them wise and nurturing. I am thrilled to have these surrogate parents, especially since my own mom and dad are long departed. This is not to say I do not have disagreements with my in-laws, but rather that I am very glad to have them in my life and I miss them when we are apart for a time.

So it is easy for me to sympathize with Moses. His own parents seem to be long dead. At least the book of Exodus does not give us any hint of their whereabouts following Moses' adoption into Pharaoh's court. Upon his return to Egypt he does meet up with his brother and sister, Aaron and Miriam, but their parents remain unmentioned. To complicate matters for Moses, his adoptive grandfather Pharaoh is also dead—a necessary precondition for his return to Egypt. His adoptive mother is, like his own birth parents, simply not mentioned as being alive after Moses' years as a shepherd in the wilderness. She is not there either to root for or agin' him during his contest with Pharaoh for the freedom of the Israelites.

Moses' blood family is limited to his siblings. But he also has a wife and a father-in-law. We have already met both his wife, Tzipporah, and his father-in-law, Jethro, also called Reuel, in earlier chapters. When we last saw Tzipporah she had bloodied her hands with a circumcision flint and then walked off the stage, seemingly for the duration. Likewise Jethro, who when we last saw him had given Moses permission to return to Egypt to carry out God's mission; Jethro, too, has been waiting in the wings.

Now that Pharaoh has been defeated, now that the Jews have come out of Egypt, now that Israel has crossed the Reed Sea on dry land, now that Amalek has been defeated, now is the time for Jethro to return to the stage. Moses, for his part, is as happy to see his father-in-law as I am to see mine.

> The priest of Midian, Jethro, Moses' father-in-law, heard of all that the Lord had done for Moses and for his people Israel, that God had taken Israel out of Egypt. So Jethro, Moses' father-in-law, took Tzipporah, Moses' wife after she had been sent away, and her two sons. One of them was named Gershom—for he said I was a stranger in a foreign land. And one of them was named Eliezer— for the God of my father came to my help and rescued me from Pharaoh's sword.
>
> So Jethro, Moses' father-in-law, came to Moses with his wife and his sons, to the wilderness where he was encamped at the mountain of God. . . . Moses went out to greet his father-in-law. They bowed

and he kissed him, and each asked the other's well-being. . . . Jethro was thrilled about all the good that God had done for the Israelites, whom God had saved from the hand of Egypt. Jethro said, "Blessed be God . . . now I know that God is greater than all the gods. . . ."

Moses' father-in-law, Jethro, took a burnt offering and sacrificed to the Lord. Then Aaron and all the elders of Israel came to break bread with Moses' father-in-law before the Lord. (Exod. 18:1–12)

And did we mention that Moses had a father-in-law? Exodus here clubs us over the head with the relationship, not, I suspect, without cause. We have seen Moses bear the burden of leading Israel and intermediating for them before God. Surely Moses knows that the ultimate responsibility for these myriads of escaped slaves lies with God. Yet Moses cannot help but feel that he and he alone of human beings must carry them through the wilderness. There is a poignant moment in the Book of Numbers when Moses plaintively asks God, "Why have You placed the load of this entire people upon me? Did I conceive all these people? Did I give birth to them that You say to me, 'Carry them in your bosom like the wet-nurse carries the suckling'?" (Num. 11:11–12). Moses is tired from his years as a fugitive, his years as a shepherd, the stress of battling Pharaoh, of pleading with God and of pleading with Israel. He has only shared the burden with his brother, Aaron, and even that was not an equal partnership. With Aaron, you will recall, Moses was the "god" and Aaron his "prophet."

At the battle of Amalek, just concluded, Moses was able to share some of his leadership. He had Joshua act the general. Joshua was further delegated to choose platoon leaders. Moses went even farther in quite literally receiving support from Aaron and Hur. Yet in every one of these instances of power-sharing, Moses remained an unequal compatriot. He was unquestionably the leader, the man calling the shots, the one on whom responsibility devolved in the end. He might well have had Harry Truman's little sign emblazoned on his godly staff. Instead of God's holy name it could have read, "the shekel stops here."

It is no small thing, then, for Moses to see Jethro appear: Jethro his father-in-law, Jethro his elder, Jethro who is more experienced in leadership, older, wiser. Moses is overjoyed and relieved to have this father figure enter the scene once more and help his son-in-law learn to bear the burdens of leadership for the long haul through the wilderness. Their very greeting is instructive in this regard. Again, it is the ancient rabbis who appreciated the lessons learned, as early as the second century. They begin with the last words of Scripture that we quoted above, "with Moses' father-in-law before the Lord." Why, ask the rabbis, does Exodus invoke "before the Lord"? This teaches, they tell us, that when one receives a colleague in greeting, it is as though one receives the very Presence of the Lord. To translate this into modern English, Jethro's appearance on the scene was perceived by Moses and the Israelites as a manifestation of divine grace.

But there is more, for those same rabbis comment on the very etiquette of the greeting offered between Moses and Jethro. Our text reads somewhat ambiguously, "they bowed and he kissed him." We do not know who bowed to whom or who kissed whom, the rabbis observe. Yet Scripture does tell us "each asked the other's well-being." By a quirk of the Hebrew pronouns the rabbis infer that it was Moses who initiated the gestures. This, they say, is appropriate etiquette, a man should always be prepared to honor his father-in-law. But the rabbis take this even farther, for they astutely point out that "each asked the other's well-being" teaches an even greater lesson.

"Great is peace and well-being," say the second-century sages, "it even takes precedence over the praise of the Blessed Holy One. For when Moses greeted Jethro he did not begin by recounting the exodus from Egypt, nor alluding to the Ten Commandments, nor by singing of the splitting of the Reed Sea, nor with tales of the manna nor the quails. No, Moses began by asking after Jethro's well-being and only afterward was everything else rehearsed. Because peace and well-being settle the mind and allow it to do everything else."

Wise men, those, who understood that both Jethro and Moses would find relief in this reunion. For Moses, the relief was that his trusted father-in-law was again on the scene. Moses had an adult, as it were, to look up to and share leadership with. For his part, Jethro was relieved to see Moses because Jethro was a father and grandfather. He had worried terribly over what it had meant when Moses sent Tzipporah and the boys back to Midian when he went down to Egypt. Indeed, the ancient rabbis worried for Jethro and Tzipporah, particularly since a verse of our Exodus narrative gave them pause. We read that Jethro came and found Moses, and brought Tzipporah with him. Scripture describes her as "Moses' wife after she had been sent away."

In the late first century, Rabbi Joshua inferred from this identification that she had been sent away by means of a divorce document. He quotes Deuteronomy 24:1, where the same "sent away" is found, as his support. There, the very topic is divorce, so he has made a fair linguistic inference about the meaning of this phrase. Further, I suspect that Rabbi Joshua may be anachronizing onto Moses the custom in rabbinic times of men leaving divorce documents for their wives when they went off to battle. That way, if he were missing in action, the wife did not remain forever tied to her possibly dead husband and could get on with her life. According to Rabbi Joshua then, we may understand Moses' attitude to Tzipporah in one of two ways. Either he wished to be rid of her and used his mission as the occasion, or he loved her enough to provide for her should his mission fail.

Rabbi Joshua was not the only first-century rabbi to speak his mind on the meaning of this verse. Rabbi Elazar of the town of Modiin suggests that Tzipporah had not been divorced, rather that Moses sent her back to her own father at the explicit command of God. This word came when Aaron met them for the first time and then advised his brother not to let them come to Egypt. "It is bad enough we worry about those who are already there enslaved. Do not subject your own family to needless danger," Moses' brother advised. In response, Moses sent her back to her father. She and the boys patiently awaited God's deliverance of husband and father. As a thirteenth-century commentary poignantly remarks, she never despaired of his return.

Yet another commentary, from the same era, attributes even greater strength to Tzipporah during the period of her abandonment. While Moses was in Egypt, the Zohar points out, Tzipporah was a single mother. Alone, she raised her two sons without any help from their father. Thus she is rewarded, for when Scripture speaks of them it tells us that Jethro and Tzipporah "and her two sons" came to greet Moses. "Her two sons" is what Exodus calls them rather than identifying them as Moses' two sons. The compliment not only pays homage to Tzipporah's efforts at mothering during a difficult time in her life but also to her faith in Moses and his mission to the Israelites. She carries her burden of family in Midian, while he carries his of Israel in Egypt.

So Jethro comes *en famille* to reunite with Moses after the Exodus. We know so little about what really happened during the time—perhaps a year—that Moses was on his dangerous mission of deliverance. In fact, Jethro himself may know very little and be dependent upon Moses to fill him in on the scoop. Nevertheless, Jethro must have heard something about the Exodus, for he knew to depart Midian and meet Moses. The Bible tells us, "Jethro, Moses' father-in-law, heard of all that the Lord had done for Moses and for his people Israel, that God had taken Israel out of Egypt." We have spent almost an entire book studying the various miracles and interventions into history and nature that God performed on behalf of the Israelites during this period. It is, in fact, remarkable to recall that *all* of these amazing events are reported to have occurred within a relatively short time span.

The rabbis of old conjecture as to what was the precipitative event. What was it that Jethro heard that brought him and his daughter and grandsons away from the relative safety of the flocks of Midian and into the wilderness searching for the Israelites? The same two rabbis who debated above, Rabbi Joshua and Rabbi Elazar of Modiin, debate this point, too. Rabbi Joshua supposes that it was the recent victory over Amalek that Jethro heard about. Joshua offers as his proof the juxtaposition of the report of the battle with the arrival of Jethro on the scene. I would add that Jethro has a great deal to gain by the defeat of the marauding Amalekites. If they prey on weak bands, then Midianite shepherds might well be a target for them. Moses' victory over Amalek may have been a signal event for Jethro and his folk. Otherwise he might have been forced into an uneasy alliance with Amalek in order to protect his own flocks and folk (see Judges, chapter six). No wonder he comes to greet Moses and the Israelites.

Rabbi Elazar, however, takes an entirely different stance on Jethro's arrival. Rabbi Elazar knows full well that the meeting takes place "at the mountain of God," which is to say the same mountain where Moses originally received his charge from God: Mount

Horeb, a.k.a. Mount Sinai. The appearance of Mount Sinai here, along with its importance in the immediately subsequent narratives of Exodus, leads Rabbi Elazar to invert the sequence of events. Here, Rabbi Elazar is joined by most modern scholars who suggest that the actual chronological order of the narrative seems to require that this reunion should take place *after* the Revelation at Sinai and the giving of the Ten Commandments. While I do not think it particularly affects our reading of the story to view it as Scripture presents it, Rabbi Elazar has a nice touch. He offers us a Jethro who cares about the covenant. Only when Jethro hears that God has given Israel the Torah does he come with his family to join the Israelites in the wilderness. Indeed, one very late commentary even suggests that Jethro converted to Judaism when he showed up.

Still other rabbis of old join the fray of interpretation. Rabbi Eliezer (not to be confused with Rabbi Elazar) suggested that Jethro came out to greet the Israelites when he heard about the parting of the Reed Sea. Rabbi Shimeon suggested that it was the manna which did the trick. Rabbi Yose suggested that it was the cloud of glory that God had sent to accompany the Israelites and shield them from harm.

One very late midrash even cleverly advances the theory that Jethro thought that all of those miracles were impressive, but what really impressed him was yet something else all together. This last source offers personal rather than national redemption as the cause of Jethro's amazement. What he heard, it suggests, is that God had cured Moses' speech defect. This is no small comment. What Jethro rejoices over is not only that his son-in-law can express himself more easily, though that would have been miracle enough. I think this midrash focuses on the nature of God's miracles. For all the other rabbis speak of national redemption. Here we see a God who cares enough to affect individual redemption. The possibility of a God who acts not only for most favored nations but also heals the individual—this is the possibility that Jethro feels moved to explore. He rejoices at both the actual cure of Moses' speech impediment and the ascent to leadership that the cure affected.

We will see in a moment, as we continue reading the Exodus narrative, that the concern of this loving father-in-law for his surrogate son is precisely about the interaction with God and the toll that role

takes on Moses. For Moses is not only the husband of Jethro's daughter and the father of his grandchildren; Moses is also Jethro's friend and, in the ways of God, his teacher. The two men share a rich relationship, they learn from one another. So Jethro can say "Blessed be God ... now I know that God is greater than all the gods. . . ." In the ninth century the rabbis note that it is as though Jethro, priest of Midian, had said, "There isn't an idol I haven't worshiped. Yet I haven't found a god that can hold a candle to the God of Israel. 'Now I know that God is greater than all the gods. . . .'"

For his part, Jethro not only learns, he teaches. A certain Rabbi Pappias, who lived at the end of the first century, remarks that this passage does not speak well of the Israelites. "There were 600,000 Israelites there and not one of them offered blessings of God until Jethro came along and taught them. He came along and praised the Omnipresent and said, 'Blessed be God.'" As we will see, it was not just Israel whom Jethro instructed. When he saw how things were being done, he had some things to teach his son-in-law, too.

As it happened, the next day Moses sat as judge for the people. They stood over Moses from morning until night. When Moses' father-in-law saw all that he had to do for the people, he asked, "What is it you do for these people? Why do you sit alone with all the people assembled before you from morning until night?"

Moses replied to his father-in-law, "I judge between one person and another when the people come to seek God's judgment. When they have a legal matter they come to me and I make known God's laws and teachings."

But Moses' father-in-law responded, "What you are doing is not good. It is too hard for you, you cannot do it alone. Both you and the people with you will be worn out. Now let me give you advice; listen to me, that God may be with you. You represent the people to God and bring their legal matters to God. You have to make them aware of the laws and the teachings, to make them know the road to travel, what they should do. So look among all the people for men of power who fear God, honest men who hate graft—set them up as magistrates of thousands, magistrates of hundreds, magistrates of fifties, magistrates of tens. Let them judge the people all the time and only bring you the important cases. The

smaller matters they shall judge. It will be easier on you if they share the burden with you . . . then all this people can return to their homes in peace."

Moses heeded his father-in-law's advice and did all that he had suggested. Moses chose powerful men from all of Israel and installed them as heads of the people . . . then Moses sent his father-in-law on his journey back to his own land. (Exod. 18:13–27)

Thank God for fathers-in-law, or perhaps in this case we should refer to Jethro by the title Father in Law. Jethro has acted as Moses' "judicial procedure" professor and earned the title. He not only sees Moses' exhaustion at attempting to constantly mediate between the Jews and God, but also his frustration at attempting to mediate or adjudicate every conflict. It is simply too much for any one man to do and Jethro tells Moses so.

Moses was so swamped that had Jethro not intervened, Moses might still be hearing cases today! As father-in-law, Jethro had a decided advantage. Moses would not refuse him a hearing of advice. And since it was clear that his father-in-law was acting out of concern for Moses' own best interests, as well as those of his wife and children, Moses was inclined to agree. No one person should be expected to carry the burdens of the entire nation. Moses was able to gratefully accept a suggestion that would bring him relief.

But Jethro's idea was better than just that, for it brought judicial relief as well. Having more magistrates allowed the people to be better served. Disputes need not fester, they could be speedily resolved. More judges, in this case, resulted in more justice all around. As Jethro pointed out, if Moses shared the burden, then everyone could go home in peace. Rabbi Simai commented in the second century that if true justice was achieved and a fair sentence was reached the result would be peace between the litigants. This is no slight achievement.

Yet Moses achieves more than a clear court calendar in this procedure. As we saw in our last chapter, he was now obligated to share the burdens of leadership not only for relief, but precisely because sharing was, in and of itself, good leadership. More people needed to be involved in the day-to-day responsibilities of leadership. The system that Jethro proposes spreads the magistracy among a broad swath of the population. Working from the 600,000 figure so often associated with the Exodus, the second-century commentary on this passage reckons Moses is charged with 78,600 judicial appointments. That is most definitely burden-sharing on a large scale.

The more vested these new leaders were, the more likely the nation as a whole was to succeed. Minimally, shared leadership served to quiet those who might otherwise complain. Being given responsibility tends to require a different perspective from those who bear it. If one has charge of a group of ten or fifty or one hundred, one may well speak out on their behalf. But one may also have to endure some of their carping. Having been on the receiving end of whining often teaches stoicism.

Indeed, being required to act the judge teaches many important lessons beyond silence. One ideally becomes sympathetic to those whose cases are heard. The problems of the people are clarified, tensions dissipated. Further, in order to judge, one not only needs to offer a sympathetic ear to both sides, one actually needs to learn the law. An eighth-century rabbinic judge points out, "When a judge does not know well what he is supposed to, then he simply must go back and learn it." Of course, the other side of the coin is represented in rabbinic circles as well. In the twelfth century a more jaded rabbinic jurist comments, "The trouble with judging is that it leaves judges with little time to learn the law."

Even today, when law schools churn out new lawyers by the myriad every May, it takes hard work to find qualified judges. It is absolutely necessary to have judges who know the law and promote it. This is a necessary yet insufficient qualification. Jethro's own political experience serves him well here in his savvy advice to his son-in-law. He teaches Moses that law must promote stable society. Judges help keep the peace as well as teach respect for the law. When the social system is based on what is perceived to be God's law, the role of judge reaches into the religious and spiritual realms as well. Choosing good judges is no easy task, so Jethro stands at the ready for Moses. He not only suggests a judicial structure but recommends appropriate qualifications, too.

Before we discuss those qualifications, mention of God's law requires a pause to marvel at how the outsider, Jethro, is given credit for the foundations of the Israelite legal system. One might well have expected, as was the case for the *content* of the law, that God should be the One to instruct Moses. A fragmentary second-century commentary to this passage takes up this theme. It notes:

> Jethro was beloved, for the Omnipresent allowed him to present this structure. It would have been apposite for God to have commanded this to Moses at the outset. But it was accomplished in this particular fashion in order to demonstrate Jethro's greatness to Moses and to all Israel—so that they could say how great Jethro was in that God agreed with his suggestion. And for his part, Jethro was careful to suggest it to Moses provisionally, only if God did, in fact, agree with him. As it is written (Exod. 18:23), "If you do this thing, and if God so commands it, then you will succeed."

Moses did succeed. His system of jurisprudence continues to influence our Western courts to this very day. As such, we still can learn from him and from his father-in-law about what qualifies a person to be a good judge. In our passage Jethro suggests the judges be "men of power who fear God, honest men who hate graft." Much later, in the Book of Deuteronomy, it is commanded that judges be charged, "When hearing a case between your brethren, judge justly whether it be each person, his fellow, or an alien. Do not show favoritism in judgment, hear the small as the great. Do not fear anyone, for judgment is God's" (Deut. 1:16–17). Even later, more advice is given, "They must judge the people justly. They may not bend justice nor show favoritism, they cannot take bribes, for bribery blinds the eyes even of sages and makes the words of the righteous twisted. Pursue justice by just means . . ." (Deut. 16:18–20).

These latter passages from Deuteronomy have generated volumes of rabbinic commentary over the centuries. But it will suffice for our purposes to look only at our Exodus passage and its implications. Jethro is no fool. He understands that judges must be men "of power." This phrase itself is open to a great deal of interpretation, for the term in Hebrew has very clear military implications: Men of power are warriors. But I do not think that Jethro is suggesting that a military tribunal become the norm for the nation. Although the term is martial, the implication is not. What Jethro is suggesting is a judiciary that is militant in its pursuit of justice. Their power comes from being wholly independent. The more power they have, the less likely they are to bend to interest groups or individuals with clout.

I remarked above that Jethro's advice about judges also had religious and social overtones. It is not surprising, then, to find a medieval commentary suggest that men of power means individuals who have gained strength through their performance of public works. This is not to suggest that, like Sir Lancelot, virtue brings strength, but rather that the ongoing engagement with the community and the habituation to community service brings its own forms of power. This is the power of communal recognition that the judge cares about the community and is vested in it. The ideal judge is partial to the community and its ideals even as that same judge is impartial to those who stand as litigants before him.

In the second century the rabbis took a different approach to the passage of Exodus. They were more schooled, perhaps, in Realpolitik. So Rabbi Joshua comments, "Men of power refers to the rich members of the community. They are not tempted by bribery." But his colleague, Rabbi Elazar demurs, "Men of power refers to people one can trust to be indifferent to wealth so that they are not subject to bribery." Both types, God willing, serve to make up an honest judiciary. As yet another early commentary points out, the best judges are those who share the virtues of wisdom, fear of God, humility, indifference to wealth, love of truth, and love of humanity. These judges who are men and women of good reputation, it is they whom we would still have judge us today.

All this and more are the lessons that Moses has learned from his father-in-law's visit. But Moses is a great teacher, and so he teaches us yet one final lesson—a lesson of family dynamics—before he goes on to assume his greatest role yet. Once Jethro has said his piece, Moses makes it clear that he has not only heard his father-in-law but will implement his advice with God's concurrence. Their mutual respect and admiration noted, Jethro is sent on his way. Yes, it is good to have the in-laws visit, but every visit must have its end. Moses has Jethro return to Midian.

This passage is not without some ambiguity, for it is a tricky thing to take leave of the in-laws and remain on good terms. The rabbis who commented on this passage in the second century were surely also aware that in the very next chapter of the Bible, Moses would prepare to receive the Ten Commandments, which contained clear admonitions about honoring one's parents. So our friend Rabbi Joshua offers that when Moses sent Jethro on his way, he sent him off with all the honor in the world. Not to be outdone, Rabbi Elazar suggests that Moses loaded Jethro down with gifts to bring home with him. They both seem to suggest the wonderful diplomacy of Moses' leave-taking. They have Moses tell Jethro, "You gave us wonderful advice and then God concurred with your suggestions! Please stay, don't leave." But Jethro is a smart father-in-law as well as being smart about law. He says, in the rabbinic imagination, "A candle is only useful when it shines in the darkness. Here all is bright. I shall return to my own people, where I am needed."

This commentary contains both wisdom and humor. People do need to dwell where they feel needed. Jethro has worn out his welcome with Israel. Having taught what he could, it is time to move on. But the rabbinic imagery is cute, Jethro is the candle lighting the darkness. He is the elderly father-in-law telling his son-in-law, I'll just go home and sit there in the dark.

However we may read this passage, Moses has achieved a great deal with Jethro's good advice. He has expanded the base of leadership to a wide cross-section of Israelites. He has instituted a justice system that alleviates the crowded court calendars. He has taken the crushing burden off of his own shoulders and shared it appropriately. He has brought the group of ragtag slaves out from under the whip and taught them the value of the judicial gavel. With the power sharing effected in this episode, Moses is now ready to transform the people further. Having built the structures and leadership that will sustain them, Moses may now transform himself from liberator to legislator.

ASCENT/
DISSENT

L eadership is a tricky business. This is especially true in a democracy such as ours, where television and polling, e-mail and letter campaigns let a politician quickly know when he or she has lost touch on an issue of importance to the folks back home. It is very easy for a member of the U.S. Congress to be sucked in, as if by osmosis, to the hermetic world circumscribed by the Capital Beltway. But the specter of being voted out of office does have a sobering effect on even the most jaded politician. No amount of campaign fund-raising, no leadership role in Congress, no party support can keep one in Washington once the constituents of a home district decide on exercising the most effective form of term limit, the ballot.

The shame of losing an election forces members of Congress to lead, as it were, from behind. While a given member of that august body may have very particular ideas, and that ideology may have even served as a platform for election, pollsters and advisers constantly remind each representative that no one issue may suffice for reelection. Further, broad-based support throughout many interests is necessary to enable leadership on any one issue.

Ironically, the polls that we despise serve as a rein on the politicians we elect. Although we may complain about representatives who hew too closely to the findings of the pollsters, it is precisely those findings, to the degree that they are accurate, that make any given representative in fact be representative. Although unforeseen by the Founding Fathers, modern sampling technology serves as yet another of the checks and balances in our representative democracy. If the first nine commandments of political life in America are fund-raising, fund-raising . . . fund-raising, then the tenth commandment must read: Thou shalt not get too far ahead of your constituents.

Alas, then, for poor Moses, who had none of the benefits of modernity, including representative democracy. It was up to him to bring the people Israel into covenant with God. It was Moses' job, as it were, to play Jay, Hamilton, and Madison and to convince the confederated tribes and their leaders to assent to the constitutional document of the Israelite nation. Of course, this analogy is inapt, for it presumes federation when the closer model is that of a suzerainty treaty.

Israel's covenant with her God is a contract that presumes a beneficent autocrat who is all powerful (God) and agrees to continue to extend protection to a helpless people (Israel), who already have benefited from the suzerain's protection. That previous benefit (the Exodus and freedom from slavery) puts them in thrall to the despot.

Having put the covenantal obligation in such stark terms, it is clear that the former slaves who make up Israel will not happily assent to the covenant. It is also clear that they will rebel against both the covenant and the suzerain at the first opportunity. Moses has taken steps to bring the people into both leadership positions and contact with God. He has made them generals and judges. They have witnessed miracle upon miracle. Yet they do not, perhaps cannot, have the relationship with God that Moses has. In the process of bringing Israel to Mount Sinai, Moses has forgotten that they have never been there before. Only he is returning to Sinai. Only he has the special, prophetic relationship with God that allows him to be the intercessor.

Unfortunately, Moses' very closeness with God blinds him to the fact that he is far ahead of his constituents. He may be able to deliver to them the Ten Commandments, but in doing so he has lost sight of that other tenth commandment—of the politician. Moses is way too far ahead of his constituents. Although both God and Moses correctly see that the arrival at Sinai appears to be a unique window of opportunity for covenant-making, they somehow fail to reckon Israel's true state of readiness for the event. In the excitement of the moment Israel will assent to the proposition of being God's people, and Moses will ascend to receive the Ten Commandments. But when he lingers too long it will all fall apart, the tablets will be smashed, and the covenant will have to be struck anew.

We, too, are running too far ahead of the moment. I am already anticipating the disaster of the Golden Calf when we have just arrived at the foot of Mount Sinai. So let us watch events unfold in their proper order and allow the thunder and lightning of Revelation to dispel the shadows of failure still to come.

On the day that marked the third month since the Exodus of the Israelites from Egypt, they came to the Sinai wilderness . . . and the Israelites encamped there facing the mountain. Then Moses ascended to the Lord and God called to him from the mountain saying, "Say thus to the house of Jacob, speak to the children of Israel: 'You have seen what I have done to Egypt, how I carried you on eagles' wings and brought you to Me. Now if you listen well to My voice and observe My covenant, you shall be My treasure among all peoples, for all the earth is Mine. You shall be a kingdom of priests and a sacred nation unto Me'; these are the words that you should say to the Israelites."

So Moses went and called the elders of the people and placed before them all of these words that God had commanded him. And the people responded unanimously and said, "All that God has said, we will do!" Then Moses brought the decision of the people back to God. . . .

So God said to Moses, "Go to the people and sanctify them today and tomorrow, have them launder their clothing so that they are prepared for the third day. For on the third day God shall descend upon Mount Sinai before the eyes of all the people. Mark boundaries around the people and warn them neither to ascend the mountain nor touch its borders, for anyone who touches the mountain will surely die. . . ."

So it came to pass on the morning of the third day that there was thunder and lightning and a thick cloud upon the mountain. The sound of the shofar was very loud so that the people who were in the camp trembled. Moses led the people from the encampment toward the Lord so that they gathered at the bottom of the mountain. Mount Sinai was covered in smoke because God had descended upon it in fire. The smoke rose like smoke from an oven and the mountain trembled powerfully. The sound of the shofar continued to get stronger. Moses spoke and with sound the Lord replied to him. God descended atop Mount Sinai. God called to Moses from atop the mountain. Then Moses ascended. . . .

And all the people saw the sounds and the flames and the call of the shofar, and the mountain smoking. When the people saw this they stumbled and then stood from afar. They said to Moses, "You speak to us and we will obey, but let the Lord not speak with us lest we die!" . . . So the people stood afar while Moses approached the mist where the Lord was. . . .

So Moses ascended the mountain while the cloud was covering it. The glory of God dwelt upon Mount Sinai so that the cloud covered it for six days. God called to Moses on the seventh day from the midst of the cloud. The appearance of God's glory was like fire consuming the top of the mountain to the sight of the Israelites. Moses went into the midst of the cloud and ascended the mountain. And Moses was on the mountain for forty days and forty nights. (Exod. 19:1–20; 20:18–21; 24:15–18)

It's one helluva theophany. The appearance of God before all of Israel was an event that forever shaped human consciousness. What exactly they all saw or heard has been subjected to a great deal of debate over the centuries. Let me be clear that I am not interested in the content of the Revelation at Sinai (at least here). I would rather take the late philosopher Martin Buber's point of view that the content of the revelation was the revelation itself. What Buber was trying to express with that gnomic statement is that it makes no difference what the Ten Commandments may have been. Oh, I suppose, like everyone else, I like the Ten Commandments, they're okay. In fact, they are more than okay, they may even qualify as neat, terrific, groovy, compelling. They have served us in good stead for millennia now, adorning our courtroom walls and such. Some people even follow the Ten Commandments: murder, adultery, Sabbath Law, the whole shebang. But for most people they are either painfully obvious or utterly ignored. So the content of the commandments is not my point here, and because of that I skipped over them in my translation of the Mount Sinai episode. For those of you who simply must have them, insert numbers One through Ten between "then Moses ascended" and "all the people saw."

Don't get me wrong, the details of the law are important, very important. Those details are what distinguish Jews from Christians and generations of Jewish communities from one another. It is not my intention to disparage the Ten Commandments, far from it. They are so important that I chose to ignore them here because I cannot do them justice. To comment on the Ten Commandments requires volumes. Fortunately, those volumes have existed in Jewish libraries for centuries on end. I am interested in different stuff. So let me start with Buber's point about revelation and then turn to how Moses and Israel dealt with it.

Professor Buber's point about Mount Sinai is that God was there. The very idea, fact, if you will, that an entire nation had firsthand communion with God is astonishing enough not to need further content. Now it is true that the Israelites experienced God's miracles on their behalf through the entire Exodus. The manifestations of God through the plagues, the splitting of the Reed Sea, the manna, even the victory over Amalek—all of these were evidence of God's existence and God's providential care for Israel, the downtrodden. Yet all of those events involved some intermediation, some aspect of nature, earthly or human, to demonstrate God's presence. Presumably the Revelation at Mount Sinai, the covenant-binding event, was different. God was present, as it were, for the closing.

The Bible is strapped to represent the ineffable, that which by definition is unrepresentable. So the text resorts to standard Ancient Near Eastern conventions to manifest God's presence there with Israel. First, there is the mountain. Then, there is the fire, the lightning, the thunder, the shofar sounds, the cloud, the rolling fog, the earth tremors. All of this might be heady enough, but it is still emphatically earthbound. Each of these phenomena is natural. So the Torah opts for the supernatural when it describes the people "seeing the sounds." This moment from the Twilight Zone is meant to provoke us toward apprehending the mysterious nature of the Revelation. It is Wholly Other, as is God.

But the Bible itself seems aware of the inadequacy of desert storm imagery when describing God. Indeed, this appearance on Sinai may be favorably contrasted with another theophany that happened a few centuries later to the prophet Elijah. When he experienced God at Sinai (1 Kings 19:11–12), it is described in similar terms, but with an added coda:

> God said to Elijah, "Go forth and stand upon the mountain before God." And behold, God passed—a great and mighty wind cleaving mountains and smashing boulders before God—but God was not in the wind. And following the wind was sound, but God was not in the sound. And following the sound came fire, nor was God in the fire. Then, following the fire, a thin quiet voice . . .

Here the Bible makes it clear that God is not *in* these natural phenomena, nor should we mistake the introductory flourish with the actual arrival of the King. No, indeed, when the King of the King of Kings speaks, all that is required is the quietest whisper. God's very presence is sufficiently powerful that all of nature's fury pales before God's puissance. As a twelfth-century commentary put it, "When the Bible speaks of God as a consuming fire, it is just a way of making it possible for human imagination to apprehend the awesomeness." The difficulty of actually apprehending God is neatly captured by Rabbi Yochanan, who suggested that each and every person at

Sinai experienced the Revelation differently, "each according to what he or she could bear." And lest you think that the "he or she" is a piece of twentieth-century political correctitude, already in the second century, rabbinic commentators make clear that the appearance of God at Sinai was to both the men and women of Israel, equally.

Allow me for a moment to come back to the problem of content. I have suggested that the event itself was the content, the very idea more important than its detail. For some classical commentaries this thought is evident in an argument over just how much revelation the Israelites actually experienced. Note that when God's presence is manifest before Israel, they fear and say to Moses, "You speak to us and we will obey, but let the Lord not speak with us lest we die!" Jewish tradition debates at what point this interjection took place. For some rabbis all Ten Commandments were spoken before Israel begged Moses to intercede. Others see the shift from first person command to second person command in the grammar of the Ten Commandments as a clue. For them, the first two commandments (delivered in first person) were the substance of God's Revelation, all else was spoken by Moses. In the ninth century it was suggested that only one commandment was spoken and at the sound of God's voice, as it were, all Israel died and then were resurrected. It was at that point they thought it a good idea to ask Moses to intercede. Even more fancifully, in the nineteenth century a great Chasidic master of Rymanov in Ukraine said only the first letter of the first word of the Revelation was heard by Israel. So much for the detailed content of the Sinai revelation!

Obviously, over the long run, rabbinic commentators would make a great deal of the details of content. For rabbis (myself included), God is in the details. It is through text and history that God is manifest to Israel and to all humanity. Yet there is a very clear strain of rabbinic thought, the one I chose to focus on here, that celebrates the Presence (theophany) more than the Presents (Commandments). Seventeen hundred years ago this idea was expressed when the rabbis suggested that, at Mount Sinai, the Israelites assembled witnessed what no further revelation ever revealed. All subsequent religious literature was subsumed in that moment.

If I may invert this idea by telescoping history (and to do this we will presume an omnipresent God), everything that was ever revealed in history to God's human creatures was revealed in that moment at Sinai. As a result, the rabbis suggest that in each and every year one is obligated to perceive oneself as though he or she stood at Sinai. This formulation is neat, for it mirrors another rabbinic formulation, that in each and every generation one is obligated to perceive oneself as though he or she had participated in the Exodus. These two events are inexorably linked. There can be no revelation without first achieving freedom from slavery. There can be no covenant with God so long as there has not been first liberty from human fealty. To use the categories of the German philosopher Franz Rosenzweig, there can be no revelation without redemption.

But were they really redeemed? It is true Israel had been liberated from bondage in Egypt, but redemption is something more than a physical condition. The ancient rabbis focus on the physical as a means of getting to the metaphysical condition of the Israelites at Sinai. They astutely point out that this ragtag group of runaway slaves were in poor physical shape. They had been beaten down by their years of hard labor. There were blind, deaf, and physically handicapped Israelites among them. Yet, the rabbis suggest, at Sinai they were healed. Perhaps it would be better to suggest that it was *by* the event at Sinai that they were healed. The spiritual experience of God manifested physical healing for those who stood there.

But they remained slaves at heart. When subjected to the thunders and tremors, they feared. The second-century commentary on this passage reads "they gathered at the bottom of the mountain," to mean that they huddled there, terrified. Emma Lazarus could not have said it better, they were tired, poor, and huddled masses, yearning to breathe free. Or as a ninth-century midrash puts it, "when our ancestors stood at Mount Sinai they trembled and feared and quaked and quivered." This fear and trembling, this sickness unto death (as Danish philosopher Søren Kierkegaard might have put it) was a deterrent to covenant. No people so terrified could willingly enter into a covenantal relationship. The terror they felt at the manifestation of their God effectively precluded any real relationship. Indeed, one of the oldest commentaries on this passage notices the peculiar Hebrew of the phrase "they gathered at the bottom of the mountain," which could also be translated "beneath the mountain." That commentary states, "God suspended the mountain over them like a pot-top and said, 'If you accept the Torah, well and good. If not, this will be your burial plot.'"

This reading is absolutely brutal. It assumes that Israel needed to be threatened as though they were still truculent slaves and God was their master. Now it is true, absolutely, that Israel were slaves to God's mastery and that, perhaps, they even needed rough treatment to understand the nature of the relationship. But it is a crude covenant that is made up of such unequal partners. Part of me rebels against this reading, for it seems too harsh. I do not like to assume that a covenantal relationship may be made if one of the parties to the covenant is unwilling. But another part of me recognizes this reading as good theology. If we are to assume that God *is* a party to the covenant, then by definition that covenant must be made between wildly unequal partners. And, like it or not, Israel, even now, are merely unwilling slaves of the autocratic Master of the Universe.

Moses, for his part, may have understood all this. Working against the odds, as it were, he does what he can to bring the slaves on board and try to avoid the mutiny. At God's instruction Moses reminds the Israelites of their debt to God, "You have seen what I have done to Egypt, how I carried you on eagles' wings." They had firsthand experience of God's beneficence. While the language of "eagles' wings" may be poetic, Israel's experience of the Exodus was not literary, it was real. As Walter Cronkite would have told them, "You were there."

Moses further takes pains to gather the elders and include them as much as possible in the theophany. In the second century the rabbis point out that this care to honor the leadership of Israel and the reminder that they all have unmediated experience of God were both parts of the ways in which God and Moses sought to bring Israel into covenant willingly. And to an extent it worked. They did say, "All that God has said, we will do!" But in the end they faltered. Their enthusiasm waned as they saw and heard with their own eyes and ears the awesomeness of God. That terror-inspiring awe showed them the inequality of the covenant to which they had assented. If anything, they fell back on their old ways and assurances.

So although the time seemed ripe, the people Israel were not. When they arrived at Sinai they were united as one people, but they were not yet sufficiently mature. It is both easy and hard to appor-tion blame for what happened. On the one hand, we expect that God ought to have known better. Yet God, too, must seize the moment, especially since the covenant is with mere humans. Even God is limited in this respect. God can make a partnership with humanity that is only as strong as human nature. When humans lose courage and look elsewhere than to God, the partnership inevitably fails.

Moses, for his part, might not have known better. He may well have thought that he did all that he could. As we have seen in the previous chapters, Moses came a long way in his leadership skills. He thought he had brought Israel to the point that they were ready to approach God and the covenant. He was ahead of his con-stituency and so he, too, was wrong.

As for Israel, they were doing fine until they realized the enor-mity of the commitment that was being asked of them. Only three months after their miraculous liberation from slavery, they were asked to willingly submit to a new sovereign. Even the miracles they had witnessed had not convinced them that God was any different from Pharaoh. In a way, they did not see God, not even at Sinai. They willfully refused to see God. They asked Moses to intercede at the very first moment that they might have had an inkling of God's enormity. In fact, it was just that inkling that made them ask Moses to intercede. They were resistant to the idea of God. They wished to be freed from slavery by miracle, but to have no concomitant sense of commitment to the force that freed them.

In a word, Israel was no different from us. We, too, are resistant to the idea of God. And submission to God is even more difficult. There is almost no modern sense that such submission has anything to do with freedom. We value freedom, and so we try to keep free-dom itself unrestrained by what look like strictures. Freedom is desirable, even great. But the vigilance that freedom demands and the commitment to be a nation under God, well, that's another story entirely. Rather than willingly accept God's sovereignty, Israel at Sinai put their faith in a representative. Having relinquished their own personal responsibility for the covenant, they could rely upon human failure—their own and that of Moses. As they stood at Sinai they thrust all of the responsibility for governance, all of their own possibility for relationship with God back into Moses' lap. When they said to him, "You speak to us and we will obey, but let the Lord not speak with us lest we die," he did not understand them. What they meant was, "You speak to us so that we need not obey. For if we truly enter a covenant with God, if the Lord speaks to us with no intermediation, then if we disobey we will surely die. So better you do the speaking and we remain uncommitted."

Moses should never have been party to the bargain. He allowed the Israelites to revert to where they were before Jethro showed them how to share the burden of leadership. He allowed Israel to jump back to their persona before they fought for themselves at the battle of Amalek. He allowed them, in essence, to return to slavery. For in thrusting all of the responsibility for their well-being onto Moses, they made him another pharaoh, as it were, a human in whom they put their faith and trust. But no human can bear that burden. It is idolatry. Moses should have refused them.

So Israel focused their attentions on Moses going up the mountain as their representative instead of noticing God coming down to be with them directly. Had they given themselves over to God, they might have found redemption. Instead they relied on a human, a false god, a hope unfulfilled. When Moses tarried on the mountain they turned to another false hope. Three months was not sufficient to free them from the shackles of slavery. Quite the contrary, they merely took the opportunity to thrust Moses into a role that he was too modest or too naive to refuse. What might have been Moses' and Israel's finest hour—the theophany at Mount Sinai—became instead a debacle. At the moment of their election, Israel chose neither Moses nor God.

> When the people saw that Moses was slow in descending from the mountain, they ganged up on Aaron and demanded of him, "Arise, make us a god who will go before us! We do not know what happened to him, this Moses, the man who took us up out of the land of Egypt."
>
> Then Aaron said to them, "Remove the golden rings in your wives' and sons' and daughters' ears and bring them to me." So all

the people removed the golden rings from their ears and brought them to Aaron. He took them from their hands and cast them in a mold and fashioned them into a molten calf.

They then proclaimed, "This is your god, O Israel, who took you up out of the land of Egypt!" (Exod. 32:1–4)

THE
ROAD TO
REDEMPTION

Needless to say, God was enraged, furious. The irony, no, the temerity of Israel was that while Moses was atop Mount Sinai getting the Ten Commandments, Israel was below, sinning. The Ten Commandments opened with "I am the Lord your God who brought you out of the land of Egypt," and the Israelites effectively responded by proclaiming of the Golden Calf, "This is your god, O Israel, who took you up out of the land of Egypt." In case that were not enough, as God was proclaiming "Thou shalt have no other gods," Israel was busy instructing Moses' brother, Aaron, "Arise, make us a god who will go before us."

Is it any wonder that God was livid? God instructs Moses, "Go ye, down, for thine people whom thou tooketh up from the land of Egypt hath abased themselves!" (Well, I am not so sure God's Hebrew was quite that King Jamesy, but the murderous intent of the final verb is all too clear.)

Verbs aside, it is God's use of pronomial adjective that is of interest. God tells Moses that Israel is "thine people whom thou took up." As it were, God temporarily washes his hands of the people Israel. Like the midrash points out, when a child gets in trouble one parent will say to the other, "Look what *your* child did." God disowns Israel and makes the sinners out to be the people of Moses, no longer the people of God. This is a not unreasonable action given that Israel has disowned God in favor of worshiping the work of their own hands.

Lashing out against the grossness of Israel's betrayal, God reacts very much like a furious parent. For even as God's anger is turned against a deserving Israel, God relies on Moses to run interference for Israel. Already the dynamic between God and Moses is clear. Let us read how the Bible tells it and then see what we can make of it.

God said to Moses, "I have seen how this is a stiff-necked people. Now, allow Me to get really angry with them and consume them. Then I will make you a great nation."

But Moses prayed to his Lord God and said, "Why, God, let Your anger burn against Your people whom You took out of the land of Egypt with great power and a strong hand? Why allow the Egyptians to say 'He took them out with evil purpose to kill them in the mountains and consume them from the face of the earth.' Turn from Your burning anger and show regret for the evil You wished to do to Your people. Recall Abraham, Isaac, and Israel, Your servants to whom You vowed by Your self when You told them 'I will make your offspring as plentiful as the stars in the sky and I shall give all this land to your offspring as a permanent possession.'"

So God regretted the evil God had planned to do against His people. Then Moses turned and descended from the mountain with the two tablets of Testimony in hand—tablets written on both sides, this way and that way were they written. The tablets were the creation of the Lord, the writing was the Lord's writing, inscribed upon the tablets. . . .

But when Moses drew near to the encampment and saw the calf and the tambourines he was furious. He flung the tablets from his hands and shattered them at the bottom of the mountain. He took the calf they had made and burnt it in fire then ground it to dust and scattered it upon the water. . . . (Exod. 32:9–20)

They take turns. First God gets angry and Moses assuages God. Then Moses gets angry and lashes out. When it is God who is angry, God gives Moses verbal clues how to react. This is like an old married couple who react to misbehavior of the children. First, God says to Moses, "Go down, for your people whom you took up out of Egypt . . ." We have already commented on God's use of "your" with Moses. But the Talmud notes that even "Go down" plays to the same dynamic. It comments that God is telling Moses, "go down from your greatness, your leadership has failed. I only gave you greatness for the sake of leading Israel and now they are sinning." This is a dynamic of blame and guilt. Like one spouse who blames the other for the children's failures, the Talmud imagines God guilting Moses into whipping Israel back into shape. It is as though God had said to Moses, "It's your fault they have betrayed me with the Golden Calf. Go down and fix it."

Another reading from the twelfth century sees God's words as a goad to Moses to be strong with Israel. "Go down," means get down on them, be tough. They have rebelled and now they need a whipping. In each of these readings God is urging Moses to be the one to act against Israel. But Scripture makes it very clear that if God urges Moses to act, it is to contain God's own murderous rage. It is one thing if Moses acts out against Israel, for Moses is human and can inflict only limited damage. If God were to lash out, the damage might be incalculable. Note that God says to Moses, "Now, allow Me to get really angry with them and consume them." The same twelfth-century midrash asks incredulously, "What, was Moses holding God back that God asks, 'allow Me'?" The point is well taken. What possible permission could the Creator of the Universe need from a human to act in any way God might see fit? When has God ever been so limited?

The midrash appreciates the subtlety of the verse. Why would God say to Moses "allow Me" if it were not to give Moses a clue that

God would welcome intercession on Israel's behalf. Indeed, Moses is a canny prophet who listens well to God. From the very threats God fulminates, Moses builds a case on behalf of Israel. God says, "I will make you a great nation." Moses is not only humble, he is wise. Moses recalls that God has made such a promise before, to Abraham, in virtually the same words. So Moses trots out the promises God made to the patriarchs as part of his response to God. Further, Moses uses a strong verb when he tells God to "regret" the evil. This is the same verb that God used way back in the time of Noah. God "regretted" creating humanity and flooded the earth; destroying all of humanity but for one family. As it were, God has now threatened to do the same again with Israel and Moses. But Moses reminds God that such "regret" is far too extreme. God already made a covenant with humanity at the time of Noah's flood not to lash out that way again. Now God must honor the covenant with Israel, the very covenant made on Mount Sinai.

Moses does not rely on this alone. He is all too aware that Israel has just broken that covenant and thus has committed an offense that may justly be capital in God's eyes. So Moses, still acting the part of spouse protecting the children, plays the "what will the neighbors think" trump card. Moses reminds God that after all of the miracles in Egypt, the strong hand and the outstretched arm, if God destroys Israel now, the Egyptians will get the wrong idea. All in all, Moses' handling of God at this juncture is stellar, a bravura performance. Moses resists God's blandishment to become a new nation and instead follows God's hint to mollify. Finally, God is calmed down enough that Moses can descend with the precious tablets of the Ten Commandments, the very tablets of testimony to the covenant Israel has just broken.

We should appreciate the lesson of parenting and leadership taught at this seminal juncture in Israelite history. Yes, people will fail. Yes, egregious errors will take place. Yes, God will react in anger against sin. Yes, God will seek to punish severely, with rampant destruction. But God will find room to be convinced otherwise. God will hear the arguments against such behavior. God will change. This idea that God might change is not only important as theology, it is important as a lesson to humanity.

Having the power and the justification need not necessarily require wanton destruction. Measured response is called for instead. If God omnipotent can be convinced to reconsider acting out in anger, surely humans should learn the same lesson. As God did with Moses, human leaders also need to have a sounding board to preclude them from regretting their actions later. The term we use here, "regret," is also variously translated as "to be sorry" or again as "renounce." It is better to regret angry action before it happens and to renounce it than to be sorry for it after the fact. This is an essential lesson for both leadership and parenting alike. The interaction of God and Moses at Sinai serves as a powerful teacher. Might is not sufficient, the voice of reason must prevail—even when the voice of reason is but human and the might is God's.

As for Moses, his case having been won, he now descends to behold what God had complained of to him. The text makes it clear that Moses' own anger goes beyond reason into rage. Moses is carrying the tablets of testimony, the Ten Commandments. In detail, Scripture elaborates on their miraculous nature. Written by God, an autograph! Written on both sides, this way and that. The midrash runs with the miracle implied and infers that the letters on the tablets were incised all the way through the stone, yet whichever way one held the tablets they were legible—no mirror images for the one standing behind the tablets! Yet miraculous as they were, Moses shatters the tablets when he sees the Israelites worshiping the calf.

The description of their worship is succinct. They have tambourines, much as they did when they sang to God for their deliverance at the Reed Sea. So, minimally, Moses is enraged at the ingratitude, the misplacement of their affections. Elsewhere in Scripture and throughout rabbinic interpretations we are led to believe that the worship of the calf also involved sexual misconduct. They very much so "have abased themselves" in their service of the Golden Calf. So Moses, now aware that he has averted total disaster, can measure his own human response. He goes ballistic.

That Moses destroys the Ten Commandments, grinds the Calf to dust, and casts it on the water is bad enough. But I confess I have left out the really gruesome part of his reaction to Israel's betrayal. First, he forces the sinners to drink the water now infused with the physical evidence of their sin—the gold dust. Then, he gathers his own tribal members, the Levites, to him with the battle cry, "All those for God, join me!" Together, they slaughter three thousand Israelites by sword. Only then does Moses' own rage abate. This extraordinary reaction is, nevertheless, a measured response. Moses has saved the entire people Israel from God's wrath. He has demurred from becoming the seed of a new people in place of Israel. But Moses recognizes that for all of his beseechment of God on Israel's behalf, they must not go unpunished. The sin of the Golden Calf is egregious.

Again, Moses' partnership with God is admirable. Even as Moses keeps God from destroying all of Israel, Moses does punish them severely. Moses takes the responsibility for their punishment upon himself. He accepts responsibility for Israel's failure toward God and so equally accepts responsibility for punishing them. In so doing, he regains his leadership of Israel, which had broken away from him, and his role as their intercessor before God. Even as he sets them to the sword, Israel must realize that Moses has averted a much greater disaster. Nor can they fail to be awed by the potent symbol of the broken tablets.

What should have been the greatest treasure Israel could possess, the covenant written by God, now becomes their perennial rebuke. The midrash imagines that the broken tablets were kept in the ark of the covenant alongside the second set of tablets, the ones that Moses will hew when he once more climbs the mountain. This symbol of failure, of disobedience, of loss of innocence, of irresponsibility is a powerful incentive to the keeping of a renewed or renegotiated covenant. If I may draw a metaphor from the prophet Hosea, it is as though Israel had been unfaithful in her marriage to God. As it were, the marriage contract had been torn up in rage. Now its tatters hang framed on the wall of the bedroom with the remarriage document. Neither partner can see the fragments without a reminder of both the guilt and the fragility of the union. Ideally, without becoming too mired in guilt, the shattered tablets become a sign of the wonderful second chance.

> On the next day, Moses said to the people, "You have committed a great sin. Now I shall reascend to God, perhaps I may win pardon for your sin."

When Moses returned to God he said, "This people has committed a great sin and made for themselves a god of gold. Now forgive their sin. If not, erase me from the book You have written."

God said to Moses, "I will erase from My book the one who has sinned against Me. Now go and lead the people where I have told you. . . ."

Then God said to Moses, "Carve two tablets of stone like the first ones so I may write on the tablets the words that were on the first ones which you smashed. Be ready in the morning and then ascend Mount Sinai and be there with Me in the morning on the mountaintop. . . ." So he carved two tablets of stone like the first ones. Then Moses rose early in the morning and ascended Mount Sinai as God had commanded him. He took the two tablets of stone in his hand as God descended in a cloud and was there with him. (Exod. 32:30–34; 34:1–5)

Moses presses his advantage with God. He already knows that God is inclined to forgive Israel because God allowed him to descend and inflict the punishment himself. Moses is keenly aware that he has averted the disaster of the Golden Calf—for now. But having seen God act out against Pharaoh and against Egypt, Moses knows that God holds a grudge and can continue to do so for a long, long time. Moses worries that Israel may suffer in the future, beyond any punishment he and the Levites may have inflicted. So, in a moment of absolute love for Israel and potential self-sacrifice, Moses bets everything on one hand. He says to God, as it were, "I know that I was responsible for a lapse of leadership. I accept that responsibility. I took it upon myself to punish Israel severely. I also acted out in anger in Your place. I broke the tablets of the covenant as surely as Israel herself had broken the covenant when they worshiped the calf. Now, God, it is up to You to forgive them. If You cannot do so, then I do not deserve to live. Indeed, if I cannot save Israel from Your wrath after all I have been through with both You and Israel, I am not at all sure I wish to live. So, either forgive them or wipe me out. Erase me from Your book."

First, the delicious ambiguity: Just what book is Moses referring to? Most readers, probably correctly, assume that God's book is the Book of Life and that Moses is risking his life with his insistence on

God's forgiveness of Israel. It is possible, however, that Exodus is being a bit "postmodern" here and that Moses is asking to be excised from the very Book we still read today. In any case, Moses takes a very real, if calculated, risk. His reward for that risk is manifold. First, for Israel, the covenant is redrawn as it was at first. There will be a second set of tablets and the Ten Commandments will be given to Israel after all. Second, for Moses, he is treated to another audience with the Divine Presence.

Once again, then, Moses ascends the mountain. Once again, God descends. Atop Mount Sinai, they are together. This transformative moment not only results in Israel's receiving the Ten Commandments but in Moses' personal enlightenment. He literally glows when he descends. Being there with God is what every mystic strives for. In a monotheistic religion, it is the epitome of all spiritual achievement. Of all God's human creatures, Moses alone experiences God face-to-face and survives. This is his redemption, his hope, his accomplishment. While he will live on yet another full generation, he lives in the glow of being there with God.

Years later, Moses would summarize the entirety of the experience to all of the Israelites and, so, to us. He says:

> "You have witnessed all that God did before your very eyes in the
> land of Egypt, to Pharaoh, to all his servants, and to his entire
> land. . . . You are assembled together this day before the Lord your
> God—your chiefs, your tribes, your elders, your officials, every
> person of Israel, your children, women and strangers among you,
> from the wood chopper to the water drawer—so that you may
> enter the covenant of the Lord your God and the sanctions which
> the Lord your God establishes with you today. Thus today you shall
> become God's people and God shall be your Lord, as promised to
> you and sworn to your ancestors Abraham, Isaac, and Jacob. Not
> only with you do I establish this covenant with its conditions, but
> with both those who are here today standing among us before our
> Lord God and with those who are not here with us today. . . ."
> (Deut. 29)

Moses spent forty years leading Israel through the wilderness. He endured their rebellions, their carping and bitching, their incessant whining. Moses was sustained throughout all those years by his dual encounters with God and with Israel. He has abided with his people through it all. He spoke on their behalf to Pharaoh. Having redeemed them from Egypt, Moses led them to the covenant with God at Mount Sinai. Again and again, he spoke on their behalf to God. His effectiveness as a leader may be measured by his success in bringing them God's redemption.

And Moses has abided with God. The encounter with God at Mount Sinai transformed him. Once he had stood there and watched a bush burn. Later he climbed the mountain and then climbed it once again to be there with God. Moses lived a remarkable life in the presence of the Lord: from Pharaoh's court to the wilderness of Midian, from the Reed Sea to Sinai, from the wadis of the desert to the sight of the Promised Land stretched before him. Beyond Mount Sinai there would be yet one more mountain for Moses to climb: Mount Nebo. There, he would see the land he would never enter. But he would climb to his death atop Mount Nebo secure in the knowledge that he had served his people and his God.

Just before he ascended Nebo, Moses spoke to Israel one last time. With full knowledge and acceptance of his impending death he told them, "I am 120 years old now, I can no longer come and go. Further, God has told me that I will not cross this Jordan River. It is the Lord your God who will cross before you . . . be strong and courageous, neither fear nor dread . . . for the Lord your God marches with you, God will not fail you nor abandon you" (Deut. 31).

This was the message of Moses' life. It is what he sought to teach the Israelites then and us today. Moses made the covenant with "those who are here today standing among us before our Lord God and with those who are not here with us today." The former group were the Israelites who wandered with him in the wilderness. The latter group are we who wander still, seeking leadership from Moses, our teacher. His story, as told to us in the Book of Exodus and throughout the Torah, consistently points to the power of community and of God's presence. This dual lesson is one we often resist. Our late-twentieth-century individualism makes us wary of too much community with all its strictures, even as we may emotionally acknowledge need for it. But each of us must find our community for emotional and intellectual support, and more. It is in community that we raise our families, do our jobs, define the very individuals whom we come to be.

Despite the constant lip service we offer, it is even more difficult for us to find our place with God. Each of us may be more or less comfortable with the *idea* of God. But the reality of God working in our lives is another matter entirely. The story of the Exodus, of the redemption of the Israelites from their enslavement, the story of Moses and his remarkable journey, all the parts of this amazing story point to the reality and presence of God. Acceptance of that Presence, being there with God, submission of the individual self to the power of the Redeemer, these are the lessons of the journey of Moses and the Israelites on the road to redemption.

The Five Books of Moses end by telling readers of the power of Moses as a leader of Israel, an intercessor before God, and teacher to us all, "There never again arose a prophet in Israel like Moses, whom God knew face-to-face, nor all the signs and wonders that God sent him to perform in the land of Egypt, to Pharaoh, his servants and all his land, nor the strong hand and all the awesome power that Moses displayed before the eyes of all Israel." It is this that Moses has taught us in the story of his long life and noble death: Redemption lies not in the crossing of rivers nor in the ascent of mountains, but in being there with God.

ONE
FOR
THE
ROAD

Rabbinic tradition teaches that one who quotes sources in the name of the person who first said them brings redemption to the world. This book depends upon many centuries of commentaries and regularly quotes from those ancient sources. Since this book is about redemption, although possibly a different kind, I have cited the names of the rabbis with regularity. I have not burdened this book, however, with the titles of the midrash texts from which the many sources have been drawn. This note is meant to guide interested readers to those sources and thus further the work of redemption.

All of the English translations from biblical and rabbinic sources are my own. I have carefully studied the translations of Everett Fox, *The Five Books of Moses* (Schocken Books), and happily commend it. I also have benefited immensely from Nahum Sarna's commentary to *Exodus* (Jewish Publication Society). Translations of rabbinic commentaries are now plentiful in English. However, the easiest reference collection to the midrash texts I have quoted—the very work I used—is a magisterial Hebrew collection by Menahem M. Kasher entitled *Torah Shelemah,* currently running forty-five volumes with more to come. In English I recommend Louis Ginzberg's seven-volume masterpiece *The Legends of the Jews* (Jewish Publication Society) and the English translation of Hayim N. Bialik and Y. N. Ravnitzky's justly famous *Book of Legends* (Schocken Books). Although immodest, it would be uncharacteristic of me if I did not mention my own introduction to midrash, *Reading the Book: Making the Bible a Timeless Text* (Schocken Books), and my treatment of Genesis, *The Genesis of Ethics* (Crown/Three Rivers Press).

It is the custom of medieval Hebrew scribes to complete the copying of a manuscript with an appropriate citation of Scripture. Weary of hand from all their copy work, they turn to Isaiah 35 for their closing prayer. It is my prayer, too:

> *Strengthen weary hands and bolster failing knees*
> *Tell the anxious of heart: "Be strong and do not fear,*
> *Behold your God, redress shall come, the Lord's compensation.*
> *God shall come and redeem you . . .*
> *Water shall burst forth in the wilderness, Wadis shall flow in the*
>   *desert . . .*
> *And there will be a road there, The holy road will it be called . . .*
> *The redeemed shall walk upon it, God's redeemed shall return upon it,*
> *Coming to Zion in song, Crowned with joy eternal*
> *Joy and delight now in hand. . . ."*